THE FRANKLIN'S PROLOGUE
AND TALE

D0522505

THE FRANKLIN'S PROLOGUE AND TALE

FROM THE CANTERBURY TALES

BY

GEOFFREY CHAUCER

*Revised Edition edited with Introduction,
Notes and Glossary by*

A. C. SPEARING

CAMBRIDGE
UNIVERSITY PRESS

PUBLISHED BY THE PRESS SYNDICATE OF THE UNIVERSITY OF CAMBRIDGE
The Pitt Building, Trumpington Street, Cambridge CB2 1RP, United Kingdom

CAMBRIDGE UNIVERSITY PRESS
The Edinburgh Building, Cambridge CB2 2RU, United Kingdom
40 West 20th Street, New York, NY 10011-4211, USA
10 Stamford Road, Oakleigh, Melbourne 3166, Australia

First published 1966
Twentieth printing 1993
Revised edition 1994
Third printing 1997

Printed in the United Kingdom at the University Press, Cambridge

A catalogue record for this book is available from the British Library

Library of Congress Cataloguing in Publication data

Chaucer, Geoffrey, d. 1400.
[Franklin's tale]
The Franklin's prologue and tale from the Canterbury tales / by
Geoffrey Chaucer. – Rev. ed. / edited with introduction, notes, and
glossary by A. C. Spearing.
p.   cm. – (Selected tales from Chaucer)
Includes bibliographical references (p.   ).
1. Christian pilgrims and pilgrimages – England – Canterbury – Poetry.
I. Spearing, A. C.   II. Title.   III. Series.
PR1868.F7S6   1994
821'.1–dc20   93–33752   CIP

ISBN 0 521 46694 6

The cover illustration shows a manuscript illumination depicting
Geoffrey Chaucer, reproduced by permission of The Huntington Library,
San Marino, California

CONTENTS

PREFACE

This edition of *The Franklin's Tale* was first published in 1966; some corrections were made in 1972, but after that it was reprinted without change. Chaucer studies, and studies of this Tale, have developed considerably since then, and my own view of the Tale has changed in fundamental ways. For this revised edition, the Introduction has been completely rewritten, and some relatively small changes have been made in the Notes and Glossary. The text of the Tale remains unchanged.

In addition to works mentioned in footnotes, readers may find the following helpful:

Piero Boitani and Jill Mann (eds.), *The Cambridge Chaucer Companion* (Cambridge University Press, 1986)

Helen Cooper, *Oxford Guides to Chaucer: The Canterbury Tales* (Clarendon Press, 1989)

Elaine Tuttle Hansen, *Chaucer and the Fictions of Gender* (University of California Press, 1992)

George Kane, 'The Liberating Truth: the Concept of Integrity in Chaucer's Writings', in his *Chaucer and Langland: Historical and Textual Approaches* (University of California Press, 1989)

A. J. Minnis, 'From Medieval to Renaissance: Chaucer's Position on Past Gentility', *Proceedings of the British Academy*, 72 (1986)

Derek Pearsall, *The Canterbury Tales* (Allen and Unwin, 1985)

Nigel Saul, 'Chaucer and Gentility', in *Chaucer's England:*

Literature in Historical Context, ed. Barbara Hanawalt
(University of Minnesota Press, 1992)
James Sledd, 'Dorigen's Complaint', *Modern Philology*, 45
(1947–8)
Mary F. Wack, *Love-Sickness in the Middle Ages* (University of Pennsylvania Press, 1990)

A. C. S.

Charlottesville, Virginia
June 1993

INTRODUCTION

Modern readers can enjoy *The Franklin's Tale* without acquiring any special knowledge of the age in which Chaucer lived or the materials from which he made his story. Chaucer was a marvellously gifted storyteller, and one reason why he is the only medieval English poet who has always had enthusiastic readers is that he seems to demand no more of us than to listen to the stories he tells. In doing so he speaks to us directly, calling on our everyday experience to confirm the truth of his remarks—

> By proces, *as ye knowen everichoon*,
> Men may so longe graven in a stoon
> Til som figure therinne emprented be   (157–9)

—and even anticipating our likely objections:

> Paraventure an heep of yow, ywis,
> Wol holden him a lewed man in this
> That he wol putte his wyf in jupartie.
> Herkneth the tale er ye upon hire crie.   (821–4)

Chaucer knew that he would have readers in a future beyond his control; at the end of his greatest single poem, *Troilus and Criseyde*, he addresses his 'little book', sending it out into the world, hoping that it will not be 'miswritten' or 'mismetred' by future copyists, and above all praying, wherever it may be read, 'That thow be understonde, God I biseche!' (I beseech God that you may be understood!). I do not wish to come between Chaucer and his readers, and my best hope finally is to leave them alone with *The Franklin's Tale*, members of the *ye* that Chaucer addresses; but he wanted to be understood, and our understanding, and thus our enjoyment, are enhanced by awareness of some things that stand behind the Tale and some that are implied but not stated in it. First I shall discuss the materials from which *The Franklin's Tale* was made; and this means that I must begin by asking the reader to take on trust the usefulness of information whose relevance will not emerge until later.

THE TALE AND ITS MATERIALS

As with most of the *Canterbury Tales*, the story Chaucer tells in *The Franklin's Tale* is not one he invented. Medieval literary works are nearly always based on sources outside themselves, and a basic assumption of medieval treatises on the art of poetry, the *artes poeticae* (to which I shall sometimes refer in this Introduction), is that a poem's *materia* or subject-matter will be supplied as a *donnée*, not invented by the writer himself. The situation was the opposite of that with the novel: authority was prized more highly than originality and no storyteller wished to give the impression that he was telling a new story. The core of *The Franklin's Tale* is a narrative unit known to folklorists as 'The Damsel's Rash Promise', found in many different medieval versions. As often with medieval popular stories, the oldest known versions are not European but oriental; but it is the European versions that introduce the magician. Chaucer refers to a book or books from which he is taking the tale—'the book seith thus' (141), 'as thise bookes me remembre' (571)—but we do not know for certain whether one specific version was his source. The version closest to his was written in Italian about 1336 by Giovanni Boccaccio in his *Filocolo*, a long prose romance including an episode in which a group of young aristocrats, presided over by Fiammetta, discuss questions concerning the conduct of lovers; one question is posed in a story similar to *The Franklin's Tale*. A knight called Tarolfo falls in love with a lady married to another knight. He persistently tries to attract her love, until eventually she thinks of a 'subtle trick'[1] to get rid of him: she promises to satisfy him if he can create a Maytime garden in January. Tarolfo meets an old man called Tebano gathering medicinal herbs; Tebano claims to be able to carry out the impossible task, and Tarolfo promises him half his wealth if he can. After performing elaborate spells and gathering herbs from throughout the world, Tebano succeeds. The lady and her attendants visit the garden, and she has to admit that Tarolfo has fulfilled her condition. He agrees to wait for his reward till her husband is away and the matter can be kept secret, but meanwhile her husband, noticing her unhappiness, questions her and she admits what has happened. Though she assures him, 'I would kill myself before I would do anything that would dishonour or displease you', he tells her she must keep her promise, and he will love her no less. With attendants, she returns to Tarolfo; and since she is not alone he guesses that she must have confided in her husband. The lady tells Tarolfo what her husband told her. Tarolfo, realizing that he cannot dishonour such a generous man, returns her unharmed. Now Tebano demands his reward; Tarolfo is willing to give it, but

---

[1] I quote Boccaccio's story from the translation in *Chaucer: Sources and Backgrounds*, ed. Robert P. Miller (Oxford University Press, New York, 1977).

Tebano is determined to be no less generous than he and the lady's husband, and will take nothing. The question to be discussed is which of the three men is the most generous; and Fiammetta provides an authoritative solution. Tebano only gave up material wealth, which is not a real good; Tarolfo only gave up 'his lustful desire', which is every man's duty; while the husband insisted that his wife should fulfil an oath that was not binding (being contrary to her marriage vows), and risked giving up his own honour (by being cuckolded), something that could never be recovered. Therefore, Fiammetta argues, the husband was the most generous.

Boccaccio retold this story in the 1350s, as the fifth tale on the tenth day of his famous story-collection, the *Decameron*. The two versions differ in various details; Chaucer's is closer to that in the *Filocolo*. There is no evidence that Chaucer had read the *Decameron*; it is generally thought that he had read at least part of the *Filocolo*, but that he did not possess a copy of it. So, whereas when he wrote *The Knight's Tale* he could work closely with another work of Boccaccio's (the *Teseida*), because he had brought a copy back from Italy, in *The Franklin's Tale* he was probably retelling Boccaccio's story from memory and adapting it quite freely. Apart from the narrative outline, it is easy to see how some elements in *The Franklin's Tale* are derived from others in the *Filocolo* story, as though a kaleidoscope had been shaken to produce a new pattern. The most striking is this: for the creation of a Maytime garden in January as the suitor's task, Chaucer substituted the removal of the black rocks from the coast of Brittany, but he seems to be recalling the original task ('as thise bookes me remembre') in lines

571–83, where he mentions the turn of the year from December to January as the moment when the rocks were removed and imagines what a garden would really be like at that season:

> The bittre frostes, with the sleet and reyn,
> Destroyed hath the grene in every yerd.   (578–9)

Another example of kaleidoscopic variation can be seen when Aurelius includes in his prayer to the sun-god Apollo a request that he should ask his sister Lucina, the moon, who 'folweth yow ful bisily' (379), to produce an extra high tide; this recalls Tebano's prayer to 'you, O stars, who together with the moon follow the resplendent day; and you, O most high Hecate . . .', especially since Hecate and Lucina are both names for the goddess Diana. A third example is that Boccaccio applies to Tarolfo's determined wooing the proverb that 'with persistence soft water pierces hard rock', while Chaucer applies the same saying in lines 157–9 (quoted above) to the persistence of Dorigen's friends in consoling her for Arveragus's absence. Boccaccio attributes the saying to Ovid: it occurs in his *Ars amatoria*, where Chaucer must also have read it, but it was probably its occurrence in the *Filocolo* that brought it to mind when he was writing *The Franklin's Tale*.

Chaucer never mentions that the story told by the Franklin is based on one by Boccaccio, and in concealing his debt he follows his usual practice, for nowhere in his works is Boccaccio's name mentioned. He ran little risk of detection, for in all probability Boccaccio's work and name were unknown in fourteenth-century England. In Italy Boccaccio was one of three great vernacular writers who enjoyed widespread fame during their lives and after their deaths; the other two were Dante and Petrarch, whose work Chaucer also knew and imitated in English. But he came to know the writings of these three only as a result of visits he made to Italy on royal business in 1372–3 (to Genoa and Florence) and 1378 (to Milan); probably none of his readers had shared these experiences. Beside *The Franklin's Tale* and *The Knight's Tale*, a third of Chaucer's major poems is also based on a work of Boccaccio's—*Troilus and Criseyde*, translated and adapted from Boccaccio's *Filostrato*. These three poems form a group with much in common. All three take their narratives from Boccaccio, but pretend to be drawing on different sources; all three are set not in Boccaccio's Italy or Chaucer's England but in the pagan past, as imagined by learned men of the late Middle Ages; and all three add to a story from Boccaccio philosophical questionings borrowed from Boethius's *Consolation of Philosophy*.

Boethius was a Roman philosopher and statesman born about AD 480, after the barbarians had conquered Rome. The *Consolation*, his last and most famous work, written shortly before his execution for treason in 524, is an attempt to see how far the philosophical truths available to human intelligence, without the benefit of any religious revelation, can console someone who has been unjustly toppled from high distinction to absolute ruin—Boethius's own situation. It forms a dialogue, in which Boethius himself voices objections to the way the world is run that would naturally occur to someone who has been unfairly accused and persecuted, and Lady Philosophy shows him how unreasonable his complaints are. Boethius was a Christian, but in this work he wrote as if he were a philosophically minded pagan, presumably because he wanted to provide arguments that would offer comfort to present and future readers whatever their beliefs. These arguments are always compatible with Christianity: Boethius assumed that the human mind, unaided, could reach belief in a single God and in life after death (as pagan philosophers such as Plato and Cicero had indeed done). In the Middle Ages, Boethius's *Consolation* was widely read; it meant much to Chaucer, who translated it from Latin into English. He also borrowed frequently from it in his more serious poems, and, whatever his view of its complete doctrine, the chief use made of it was as a source of philosophical arguments that could be attributed to pre-Christian pagans. In *The Franklin's Tale* the chief debt to Boethius is in Dorigen's speech about the black rocks (193–221). No such questioning of God's ordering of the universe occurs in the *Filocolo* or any other version of 'The Damsel's Rash Promise'. In the Middle Ages Christian belief was universal, and was supported by a single Church with no serious rivals, so that, as Chaucer puts it, 'hooly chirches feith in our bileve / Ne suffreth noon illusioun us to greve' (461–2). Chaucer shared this faith, but questions about the reason why evil and suffering exist—questions foreclosed by 'feith in our bileve'—intrigued and troubled him, and are raised repeatedly in his poems. That must have been one reason why he so often imagined characters from the pagan past.

Concealing his debts to Boccaccio and Boethius, Chaucer claimed that *The Franklin's Tale* had a quite different source. The Franklin's statement in his Prologue is unequivocal:

> Thise olde gentil Britouns in hir dayes
> Of diverse aventures maden layes,

7

Rimeyed in hir firste Briton tonge;
Whiche layes with hir instrumentz they songe,
Or elles redden hem for hir plesaunce,
And oon of hem have I in remembraunce,
Which I shal seyn with good wil as I kan.   (37–43)

In itself this deceptiveness about sources is a common
medieval practice. In *Troilus and Criseyde* Chaucer claimed
that his source was a non-existent Latin author called
Lollius. There Chaucer wanted to give the impression that
a narrative set in classical antiquity had an authentic
classical origin. One might expect him to do the same in
The Franklin's Tale; so why did he claim to be repeating a
Breton lay?

  In naming a Breton lay as its source, Chaucer is relating
the Tale to a specific literary genre. The earliest known
Breton lays are by Marie de France, a French poet writing
in twelfth-century England. She claims to be repeating
stories recited by Breton minstrels; it seems likely that she
was the inventor of the genre as a written form. Her lays
are short verse-romances, dealing with the adventures of
idealized knights and ladies, and often involving magic or
the supernatural. Her plots frequently have a dream-like
randomness; her lays are elegantly concise in expression,
yet charged with feelings and meanings that go far beyond
what is said. *The Franklin's Tale* does contain a large
supernatural element, yet this is not left mysterious, but is
explained in detail as 'scientific' natural magic or as illusion.
It does begin with aristocratic characters of an idealized and
typified kind, but at crucial points in the narrative these
tend to be developed in ways that incite us to take a keen
interest in them as individuals. The narrative itself, far from
unfolding like a dream, is compactly ordered. Moreover,

while Marie's lays generally take extra-marital love as the norm of interesting human relationship, Chaucer focuses attention upon the relationship of the married couple Dorigen and Arveragus. Aurelius's attempt to break up this relationship by having an affair with Dorigen is halted by his own decency; if *The Franklin's Tale* were really a Breton lay, his affair with Dorigen would probably be the emotional and imaginative centre of the work. Moreover, there is no evidence to suggest that Chaucer had actually read any Breton lays in French; the only indication of a link with the lays is found in the information about them in lines 37–43 (quoted above) and this corresponds to material in a preface attached to two English versions of lays, both surviving in a fourteenth-century manuscript written in London. It seems quite possible that Chaucer knew this very manuscript, and took from it all he knew about lays.[1]

Whether or not Chaucer knew any French lays, we can speculate as to why he claimed a Breton lay source for *The Franklin's Tale*. Some possible reasons are these. First, even though he presents magic more rationalistically than it appears in real Breton lays, he gives it a crucial role in *The Franklin's Tale*, and that makes it unusual among his poems. Of the other *Canterbury Tales*, only *The Wife of Bath's Tale* and *The Squire's Tale* include magic at all, and only the latter (which immediately precedes *The Franklin's Tale* in the collection) describes it in any detail. So Chaucer could well have felt that *The Franklin's Tale* had some affinity with a romance genre in which magic was prominent; indeed, his own scepticism about magic might have led him to regard magic as a generic feature of the Breton lay.

[1] L.H. Loomis, 'Chaucer and the Breton Lays of the Auchinleck MS', *Studies in Philology*, 38 (1941).

Second, Breton lays characteristically give special emphasis to human feelings: it is feelings that drive the action, give meaning to the characters' lives, and charge objects and settings with symbolic significance. By contrast with Boccaccio's versions of the story, which are little more than ingenious narrative machines (amplified in the *Filocolo* by a sensational treatment of magic as pagan ritual), Chaucer's version gives central importance to the characters' feelings. The longest speeches—Dorigen's address to God (193–221), her *compleynt* (682–784), and Aurelius's prayer to Apollo (359–407)—are all expressions of extreme emotion, and the whole tale focuses on the emotions underlying its events: Dorigen's longing and fear during her husband's absence in England, her suicidal grief at the thought of keeping her promise to Aurelius, and her half-mad misery (839) when it seems that she cannot avoid doing so; Aurelius's desire for Dorigen and despair of gaining her, culminating in the 'langour and ... torment furius' (429) of his prolonged love-sickness and the reckless joy with which he promises the magician an impossibly large reward; the 'wo, ... peyne, and ... distresse' (65) suffered by Arveragus at the gap in rank that initially keeps him from declaring his love, and his anguish when he feels obliged to tell Dorigen to keep her promise even though she believed when making it that it need never be fulfilled. The Clerk alone is never at the mercy of his feelings. Outward expressions of emotion occur everywhere: tears, 'sorweful sikes colde' (192), lamentations, imploring looks (285–6), 'raving' (354), swooning, turning away (339), leaping up (496), turning suddenly pale (668), kneeling in supplication or gratitude, cursing. Most of these emotions are painful; they are repeatedly associated with the fear or threat of death. Arveragus sent Dorigen word that he would soon return from England, 'Or elles hadde this sorwe hir herte slain' (168). Aurelius's response to Dorigen's demand that he remove the rocks is, 'Thanne moot I die of sodeyn deth horrible' (338), and he begs the Clerk either to relieve his suffering 'Or with a swerd that he wolde slitte his herte' (588). Aurelius assures Dorigen, 'Ye sle me giltelees for verray peyne' (646); when she learns that he has fulfilled her condition she considers suicide and lists many cases of women who 'Chees rather for to die' (712) than be dishonoured. Arveragus assures her that he 'hadde wel levere ystiked for to be' (804) than have her break her word, but warns her 'up peyne of deeth' (809) never to reveal the shame she will bring upon them both by keeping it. And Aurelius reports to the Clerk that Arveragus

> Hadde levere die in sorwe and in distresse
> Than that his wyf were of hir trouthe fals,   (924–5)

while Dorigen 'levere had lost that day hir lyf' (928) than be unfaithful to her husband.

Many of these painful feelings are treated with a certain distance or even disdain, as in Chaucer's rapid summary of Dorigen's expressions of distress at Arveragus's absence—

> For his absence wepeth she and siketh,
> As doon thise noble wives whan hem liketh.
> She moorneth, waketh, waileth, fasteth, pleyneth . . .   (145–7)

—or his callous dismissal of Aurelius's love-sickness: 'Chese he, for me, wheither he wol live or die' (414). The reason for this will be discussed later, but here I must add that it coexists with repeated emphasis on warm and

Introduction

practical sympathy among the characters for each other's sufferings. Dorigen's friends 'Conforten hire in al that ever they may' (151) when she misses her husband, begging her to join them in strolling along the coast and, when that fails, in visiting 'othere places delitables' (227), playing board-games, picnicking and dancing. Aurelius's brother puts him to bed when he finds him unconscious from unrequited love, weeps secretly for his sorrow (444), and rejoices when he thinks of the possibility of curing him by magic. When Arveragus learns of the dilemma that is troubling Dorigen, he is not angry but responds 'with glad chiere, in freendly wise', asking only, 'Is ther oght elles, Dorigen, but this?' (795–7). And it is a capacity to feel *compassioun* and *pitee* for others that leads to the competitive exercise in generosity that brings about the Tale's happy ending. The sympathy pervading the fictional world will surely encourage readers to enter sympathetically into the characters' feelings, if not always to take them seriously, and thus to share in the generous attitude of the conclusion.

This stress on human feelings, then, relates *The Franklin's Tale* to the atmosphere of Breton lays. More specifically, Marie de France's lays tend to focus on the feelings of their female characters. Marie herself is a rare example of a female medieval writer, women often play leading roles in her stories, and she takes a special interest in their roles and inner lives. In one case, indeed, she begins a tale by explaining that 'It was first called *Eliduc*, but now the name has been changed, because the adventure upon which the lay is based concerns the ladies': now, she says, it is called after the hero's wife and mistress.[1] Though Chaucer was a man, his early

[1] *The Lais of Marie de France*, trans. Glyn S. Burgess and Keith Busby (Penguin, 1986).

readers noticed the sympathy shown for women in his poems; the Scottish poet Gavin Douglas, a century after Chaucer's death, explained that when he changed the story of Virgil's *Aeneid* to put Aeneas's mistress Dido in a better light, it was because 'He was evir, God wait, all wommanis frend' (He was always, God knows, a friend to all women). Though *The Franklin's Tale* is structured by a competition in generosity among three men, on another level it is the tale of Dorigen: her feelings are at its centre, she has its longest speech, she raises its most disturbing philosophical questions, and only in the last fifty lines does interest shift from her to the three male characters. In this respect *The Franklin's Tale* differs greatly from the story Chaucer remembered from the *Filocolo*. There the wife is nameless, she says little, we learn little about her feelings, and when we are told that 'she was full of grief and melancholy' those feelings are stated, not explored. Perhaps we are not always meant to enter fully into Dorigen's extreme emotions, perhaps they involve contradictions of which she herself is unaware, but she is a character who would have appealed to Marie de France, and whose centrality in her story gives it a resemblance to a Breton lay.

A last reason why Chaucer may have described *The Franklin's Tale* as a Breton lay is the most obvious, namely that he set it in Brittany. One of the Tale's imaginative foci is the black rocks, which are not known to derive from any source. It is these that attract Dorigen's anxiety during her husband's absence; this suggests the idea of setting their removal as an impossible task to Aurelius; and this in turn is what introduces the important element of magic into the story. A chain of black rocks really exists off the Breton coast. (When my daughter was at boarding school in

Brittany, she sent a picture postcard showing them just as Chaucer describes them, though the precise place he mentions lacks cliffs from which Dorigen and her friends could have viewed them.) It might well have been the real existence of those rocks, learnt from charts or from conversation with some of the many Englishmen who had visited Brittany, that gave Chaucer the idea of a Breton setting for *The Franklin's Tale*. He filled it in with remarkably accurate topographical detail. Arveragus and Dorigen live at *Pedmark*, which is a real place, now called Penmarc'h, situated south of Brest, on a headland, surrounded by a chain of dark-coloured and dangerous rocks like those in the poem. Chaucer even seems to have known how high the spring tides were in this area, because he makes Aurelius pray that the flood tide should be at least 'five fadme' (388: about nine metres) above the rocks. The mean range of spring tides locally is such that if the flood tide were this high, the ebb tide would just cover the rocks.[1] Other details are equally accurate. Arveragus comes from Kayrrud, apparently a genuine fourteenth-century Breton place-name, phonetically spelt. Aurelius's brother has studied at Orleans, where he saw a book on natural magic belonging to a fellow-student who was supposedly studying law. In the Middle Ages young Bretons really went to Orleans university, and it really was a great academic legal centre which also had a reputation as a place where astrology and magic were studied. The Breton background to the story is thus remarkably full and coherent. Paradoxically, this very fact also makes *The Franklin's Tale* unlike a Breton lay. Though the genuine lays sometimes refer to

[1] Noted by Phyllis Hodgson (ed.), *The Franklin's Tale* (Athlone Press, 1960).

actual places in Brittany, they lack the topographical detail found in Chaucer's poem: their world is a vaguely imagined fairyland, where specific features such as the sea, castles, woods, and so on, appear and disappear as needed. The world of *The Franklin's Tale* is imagined with a solidity that is distinctively Chaucerian.

There is another way in which Chaucer changes the Breton setting to produce an effect that would have surprised Marie de France. Her lays are set in an imaginary past, where magic and Christianity coexist and the customs are those of her own time; they are unrelated to any real history. This was the normal practice among medieval storytellers, but Chaucer had a stronger historical imagination than most of his predecessors and contemporaries. He could imagine a past different from the English fourteenth-century present, and what interested him particularly, as noted above, was to imagine a pagan past, before the Christian revelation. The *Filocolo* story is set in the recent, and therefore Christian, past, yet Tebano's magic involves him in praying to pagan gods and performing pagan rituals. Chaucer, on the other hand, classicized and paganized the setting of his version as completely as he could. His first line mentions Armorica, the Roman name of Brittany, and he later parallels this by mentioning 'Briteyne' (138), thus introducing Britannia, the Roman name of England. Aurelius too is a Roman name; and such details prepare us for the pagan religion and philosophy of Dorigen's protest against the ordering of the world and Aurelius's prayer to the pagan sun-god Phoebus Apollo, with its references to his 'temple in Delphos' (405) (inaccurate though this is), and to his fellow deities Lucina, Neptune and Pluto. The world of *The Franklin's Tale* is in this way unlike that of any actual Breton lay, but, with its strange blending of medieval Brittany and classical antiquity, it is also unlike that of any other poem by Chaucer.

THE TALE AND ITS THEMES

The Franklin's Tale is a medieval courtly romance, and this means that it is a story with a meaning, devised not just to hold our attention and stir our feelings but to make us think about its larger implications. Some of these are stated explicitly; others are implicit, may or may not have been consciously intended by Chaucer, and may be drawn out differently by different readers. Moreover, because of the complex narratorial situation in *The Canterbury Tales*, with the stories and their interpretations attributed to the various pilgrims, who in turn offer different views of each other's tales, we are granted a remarkable degree of freedom to read any tale in ways that diverge from or even contradict its explicit thematic purposes. Alongside the heartfelt prayer, 'That thow be understonde, God I biseche!', may be set a line repeated several times in *The Canterbury Tales* in slightly varying forms: 'Diverse folk diversely they seide' (Different people said different things). It first occurs in *The Reeve's Prologue*, referring to the pilgrims' differing reactions to the tale just told by the Miller; it acknowledges that no reading of a tale can be unquestionable, and licenses readers to apply their own understandings to the process of interpretation—a process that will never cease until there are no more generations of readers to engage in it. I begin with the explicit themes of *The Franklin's Tale*, but even these, clearly stated though they are, can nevertheless elicit different responses from different readers.

The explicit themes are marriage, *trouthe* and *gentillesse*. On each of these topics the Tale has definite teaching to offer, in the form of moral generalizations or *sententiae*, that invite our rational assent. Medieval thinkers found it hard to justify the existence of fictional narratives that lacked an ethical purpose, and it was common for stories to be accompanied by explicit morals, whether stated by the storyteller or by his characters. In *The Franklin's Tale*, teaching on the subject of marriage, offered by the story-teller himself to his listeners or readers, appears in a digression or *diversio* running from line 89 to line 126. As happens in several *Canterbury Tales* (*The Merchant's Tale* and *The Pardoner's Tale* are other instances), the narrative has barely begun when it is halted in order to state the theme it is intended to exemplify, and only after a *diversio* of some length does it continue. Here it consists of a whole series of *sententiae*, the essence of which is stated in the *diversio*['s] opening lines:

> For o thing, sires, saufly dar I seye,
> That freendes everich oother moot obeye,
> If they wol longe holden compaignye.
> Love wol nat been constreyned by maistrye.   (89–92)

On the subject of *trouthe* the Tale's explicit teaching is the statement wrung out of Arveragus at the painful moment when Dorigen tells him that Aurelius has succeeded in performing the task which she swore would win her love, and leaves it to him to decide what to do: 'Trouthe is the hyeste thing that man may kepe' (807). The third theme of *gentillesse* is one mentioned at various points in the Tale, but we may find its doctrine summed up in the statements of Aurelius and the Clerk when each decides not to demand fulfilment of a promise:

> Thus kan a squier doon a gentil dede
> As well as kan a knight, withouten drede   (871–2)

and

> Thou art a squier and he is a knight;
> But God forbede, for his blisful might,
> But if a clerk koude doon a gentil dede
> As wel as any of yow, it is no drede!   (937–40)

Gentillesse, then, is not a matter of rank but of moral virtue. These statements are clear enough in themselves, but when we come to examine the three themes as they are embodied in the Tale, we shall find the matter less simple than it seems. In each case, the theme will open the way to further questions, to varying responses, to an uncertainty that is more troubling than simplicity and clarity, but also more interesting and more like life. Let us consider each theme separately.

Marriage

This may seem an intrusive topic, imposed on *The Franklin's Tale* as part of a thematic pattern established in a larger group of the *Canterbury Tales*. Boccaccio's version of the story, while indicating the mutual trust of husband and wife, offers no general thought about marriage, and it is easy to see why: the story of a lady's escape from the consequences of her rash promise requires no special emphasis on the ideal quality of her relationship with her husband. We need to know that they truly love each other, or his insistence on her keeping her promise would lack dramatic force, but nothing more is strictly necessary. Chaucer, however, seems determined to include more; he explains in detail the unusual agreement on which their relationship is based, and then turns aside in the *diversio* just mentioned to defend this arrangement on grounds of general principle. The arrangement is that, instead of Arveragus's assuming the dominance (*maistrie*) that usually belonged to a medieval husband, he agrees to obey Dorigen as a medieval lover was expected to obey his lady. In return, she agrees to obey him, and so each becomes servant and each master. The defence of this arrangement is that 'Love is a thing as any spirit free' (95) and hence 'wol nat been constreyned by maistrye' (92). Most twentieth-century readers of *The Franklin's Tale* have shared this view of the marriage relationship and many have felt that it was Chaucer's own, presented as his conclusion to a debate on marriage conducted in earlier tales.

The idea that a debate or discussion on marriage is embodied in parts of *The Canterbury Tales* was first put forward by G. L. Kittredge in 1912, and quickly achieved widespread acceptance.[1] According to this view, the core of the debate is to be found in four contributions, those of the Wife of Bath, the Clerk, the Merchant and the Franklin, which occur in that order in the best *Canterbury Tales* manuscripts. They are all concerned not just with marriage but with *maistrie* in marriage, a favourite topic of both learned and popular discussion in the Middle Ages. The

[1] Kittredge's article, 'Chaucer's Discussion of Marriage', *Modern Philology*, 9 (1911–12), is often reprinted in volumes of chaucer criticism. For more recent versions of the argument, see W. W. Lawrence, *Chaucer and the Canterbury Tales* (Oxford University Press, New York, 1950), and R. E. Kaske, 'Chaucer's Marriage Group', in *Chaucer the Love Poet*, ed. Jerome Mitchell and William Provost (University of Georgia Press, 1973).

Introduction

Wife of Bath offers an extreme example of female dominance. Having boasted in her Prologue that she has had five
husbands and achieved *maistrie* over them all, she tells a
tale in which a knight has imposed on him the task of
discovering what women most desire. An ugly old woman
gives him the right answer—*maistrie* or *sovereinetee*—but
only on condition that he marries her. At first her ugliness
and low birth repel him but, after she has lectured him on
the subject of *gentillesse*, he concedes *maistrie* to her, and
she turns by magic into a young, beautiful and obedient
wife. After this tale come two that are not concerned with
marriage, but the topic is then resumed by the Clerk. He
tells of a peasant girl married to a marquis; he submits her
to an appalling series of torments and humiliations, all of
which she accepts patiently; at last, recognizing her con-
stancy, he takes her back into favour. Though the Clerk
describes this as a parable showing how human beings
should endure the tests God sends them, he refers specifically to the Wife of Bath as a figure antithetical to his
heroine. *The Merchant's Tale* comes next, and is explicitly
linked with *The Clerk's Tale*. The Merchant has recently
married, he says, a wife very different from the Clerk's
patient heroine, and he tells of an old knight who, after a
lifetime of bachelor dissipation, marries a young woman
who at once deceives him. He goes blind, and she commits
adultery with a young squire in his very presence.

Close links between *The Franklin's Tale* and the three
tales just summarized will be apparent. The Franklin seems
to offer a mean between the two extremes represented by
the Wife of Bath and the Clerk: neither total dominance by
the wife nor total dominance by the husband, but a
compromise in which both are master and both servant.

Again, *The Franklin's Tale* seems to defend marriage itself against the cynicism of the Merchant's attack, repeating the basic situation of his tale—the marriage of a knight and a lady subverted by a young squire's advances—but bringing it to an unironically happy conclusion. Further, in linking *gentillesse* with marriage as themes of his tale, the Franklin returns to *The Wife of Bath's Tale*, where the knight had to learn the nature of true *gentillesse* before he could gain a happy marriage. There are other, more detailed connections among the four tales; but it does not follow from this that Chaucer intended *The Franklin's Tale* as a solution to the problem of *maistrie* in marriage raised by its predecessors. In general, it was not Chaucer's habit to offer solutions to problems; his tendency was rather to present interesting human situations and leave us to draw our own conclusions.

The Franklin's Tale begins with a situation more typical of the endings of courtly romances. A knight loves a beautiful lady from a distance and performs 'many a greet emprise' (60) to win her; she takes 'pitee' on his 'penaunce', and at last agrees to marry him. So far their relationship has belonged to the convention of *fine amour*, by which the lady is the dominant partner, the knight's 'mistress' in a literal, feudal sense. But this must end with marriage, for in medieval marriage, at least in theory, the husband rules. But this is only the beginning, for in this case the unusual arrangement mentioned above is tried; and now the *diversio* in defence and explanation of their agreement begins, its gist being, as I have said, that 'Love wol nat been constreyned by maistrye' (92). The 'debate' about marriage has been a debate about *maistrie*, with both sides seeing marriage as a struggle for power, in which either husband or wife must emerge victorious. Now it is proposed to resolve the problem by changing its terms, removing the question of dominance from marriage, and presenting it as something other than a power relationship. Women by nature desire liberty; so do men; therefore both parties to a marriage must show *pacience* and *suffraunce*—concepts that Chaucer and other medieval writers praised highly as moral and spiritual virtues. To us they may seem forms of weakness, but, when undertaken as conscious choices (as by the obedient wife in *The Clerk's Tale*), not merely as 'tolerance' based on apathy or fear, they were regarded as forms of strength:

> Pacience is an heigh vertu, certeyn,
> For it venquisseth, as thise clerkes seyn,
> Thinges that rigour sholde nevere atteyne. (101–3)

Pacience may sometimes be a prudent response to what cannot be changed:

> Lerneth to suffre, or elles, so moot I goon,
> Ye shul it lerne, wher so ye wole or noon. (105–6)

Why kick against the pricks? or, as Chaucer puts it in his short poem *Truth*, 'Be war therfore to sporne ayeyns an al' (So beware of kicking against an awl); but, when practised in the continuing relationship of marriage, *pacience* implies flexibility, sensitivity to changing circumstances—'After the time moste be temperaunce' (113: behaviour must be governed in response to occasion)—and dynamism rather than dogged endurance.[1] Most modern readers in Western Europe and the English-speaking world are likely to feel

---

[1] See Jill Mann, 'Chaucerian Themes and Style: the *Franklin's Tale*', in *The New Pelican Guide to English Literature*, ed. Boris Ford, vol. 1, Part 1 (Penguin, 1982).

that this teaching is simply correct: husband and wife should be equal partners, and power should have nothing to do with the matter. We cannot assume, though, that this would always be the medieval reaction. The normal medieval view was that a happy marriage relationship would be established, not by trying to abolish dominance, but by both parties agreeing that the husband should be dominant. The right relationship was as stated in a medieval encyclopaedia, Bartholomew the Englishman's *De proprietatibus rerum*: 'a man is the hed of a womman, as the apostil seith. Therfore a man is holde [obliged] to rule his wif, as the heed hath the cure [care] and reule of al the body.'[1] 'The apostle' is Saint Paul, whose teaching on marriage became the basis of medieval ecclesiastical doctrine. It is stated most fully in his Epistle to the Ephesians 5:22–24 (here quoted in the Douay translation of the medieval Latin Bible):

> Let women be subject to their husbands, as to the Lord:
> Because the husband is the head of the wife, as Christ is the head of the church. He is the saviour of his body.
> Therefore, as the church is subject to Christ, so also let the wives be to their husbands in all things.

The same teaching appears in *The Parson's Tale*, the orthodox penitential manual placed at the end of *The Canterbury Tales*. What Arveragus and Dorigen are praised for attempting is unquestionably well-intentioned and even noble, but it opposes ecclesiastical orthodoxy; moreover, such high ideals might not always work in practice. These noble pagans are attempting, some medieval readers might have felt, to bring back the Golden Age, the

[1] From the fourteenth-century translation by John of Trevisa, ed. M. C. Seymour (Clarendon Press, 1975), Book VI, ch. 13.

mythical period of pagan happiness when humanity lived according to nature, before *maistrie* tainted all human relations. The myth was available in many sources, both classical and medieval, and one certainly known to Chaucer, because he had translated some of it into English, was Jean de Meun's addition to the thirteenth-century *Roman de la Rose*. In the Golden Age, Jean wrote, 'All were accustomed to being equal, and no one wanted any possessions of his own. They knew well the saying . . . that love and lordship never kept each other company nor dwelt together. The one that dominates separates them. It is the same in marriages . . .'. Later Jean describes a jealous husband who 'makes himself lord over his wife, who, in turn, should not be his lady but his equal and his companion, . . . and, for his part, he should be her companion without making himself her lord or master'. Later still, an old woman affirms that 'women are born free' and that 'all women of every condition, whether girls or ladies, have a natural inclination to seek out voluntarily the roads and paths by which they might come to freedom, for they always want to gain it'.[1]

What happens to the marriage of Dorigen and Arveragus when it is tested by the course of the story could be interpreted as revealing the risky impracticability of their utopian idealism. The depth of Dorigen's affection for Arveragus is never questioned, and she is thoroughly shocked when Aurelius declares his love:

> She gan to looke upon Aurelius:
> 'Is this youre wil,' quod she, 'and sey ye thus?
> Nevere erst,' quod she, 'ne wiste I what ye mente.'   (307–9)

[1] *The Romance of the Rose*, trans. Charles Dahlberg (University Press of New England, 1983).

But instead of simply turning him away, she makes the 'rash promise' that is the core of the traditional story. Once put in the context of an ideal of marriage in which the wife retains her *libertee*, Dorigen's setting of an impossibly difficult task as the price of her love takes on a new significance: she uses her independence to behave not like a wife but like a lady in a courtly romance, who is free to establish for herself the terms on which she will grant her favour. But the shift in the nature of the task from the creation of a Maytime garden in January to the removal of the rocks from the Breton coast complicates the situation still further and hints at intriguing psychological complexities. Why *this* task? We can easily guess that it occurs to Dorigen because of her preoccupation with the danger that those rocks will wreck Arveragus's ship when he returns from England. Her protest to God about the rocks' existence ended with the wish 'that alle thise rokkes blake / Were sonken into helle for his [Arveragus's] sake!' (219–20), and now she orders Aurelius to make this wish come true. The situation is deeply paradoxical: she promises herself to her would-be lover if he will ensure the safe return of her husband, who will thus either become a cuckold or prevent her from fulfilling her promise! What is more, we are told that Dorigen sets this task not, like the *Filocolo* lady, as a rationally calculated 'subtle trick', but 'in pley' (316), as a contradictory supplement to the 'final answere' (315) she has just given. The phrase 'in pley' may be intended to shield Dorigen's motives against analysis, but twentieth-century readers have learned from Freud that jokes and slips of the tongue are especially likely to reveal hidden motives, and we may not be able to resist speculating further.

With the aid of magic, Aurelius performs the impossible task, and Dorigen is in a terrible dilemma. She considers suicide, but now her husband, who has been 'out of towne' (679) on another trip, returns once more, and she immediately takes her problem to him. In doing this, Dorigen does not follow the Tale's theory of marriage, which would surely lead her to use her *libertee* to kill herself—a noble death for a pagan, though a sin for a Christian. She acts instinctively, and instinct leads her back to the submission that would have been thought appropriate for a medieval wife. Arveragus in turn, under the pressure of this crisis, resumes his role as 'head' and instructs her what to do: 'Ye shul youre trouthe holden, by my fay!' (802). 'Shul' means something closer to 'must' than to the modern 'shall', and there are later reminders (840, 846) that Arveragus 'bad' (commanded) her to keep her promise. Thus at this crucial point *maistrie* re-enters the marriage, with an emphasis reinforced by the further paradox that Arveragus uses his *maistrie* to direct his wife to become someone else's mistress. The ideal marriage arrangement praised in the *diversio* was expressed in paradoxical terms:

> Thus hath she take hir servant and hir lord—
> Servant in love, and lord in mariage.
> Thanne was he bothe in lordshipe and servage.
> Servage? nay, but in lordshipe above . . .   (120–3)

Put into practice, it has led to paradoxes that are a matter not just of verbal play but of human suffering, *lived* contradiction. Arveragus and Dorigen are released into their happy ending by a series of acts of *gentillesse* apparently not connected with their original agreement.

This at least is one way of interpreting the theme of

marriage in *The Franklin's Tale*. Other interpretations are possible, ranging from those that find no tension at all between the Tale's theory and its practice to those that see the theory as foolishly mistaken, even heretical, from the very beginning. It would be wrong to pretend to certainty, especially on a topic of such central interest and disagreement as marriage, on which we all have our strong views. 'Diverse folk diversely they seide'; opinions that now seem enlightened might in the Middle Ages have seemed unwise, and vice versa; and one of the greatest dangers for admirers of a writer from the past is to be unable to bear to feel that he would disagree with them on any important topic.

Trouthe

Vows, promises and other forms of obligation based on the pledged word are common devices in medieval narratives; a favourite theme is the requirement to fulfil the exact wording of a promise even though the outcome may differ from what was envisaged when it was made. In *Sir Gawain and the Green Knight*, for example, the story begins with Gawain formally agreeing to an exchange of axe-strokes with the Green Knight: Gawain is to strike first, and he promises by his *trawthe* to seek his opponent a year later, at a place to be revealed only after the first blow has been struck. When Gawain slices off the Green Knight's head at a single stroke, his promise would appear to be null; but the Green Knight remains upright, retrieves his head from the floor, and tells Gawain that he must seek the Green Chapel and there receive a return blow. It is never suggested that, because Gawain thought it impossible for his opponent to survive the first axe-stroke, he is relieved of his promise to receive the second. In romances promises are a means of generating adventures, sequences of events that challenge and test the participants by their very unpredictability; but in the medieval world they did not belong only to fiction. In unruly societies where official law enforcement was unreliable, verbal pledges were often all that stood between order and chaos; the very basis of the feudal system was the public oath of loyalty between lord and vassal, and to break such an oath was to incur public shame. *Trouthe* is a general term for integrity, or fidelity to what has been pledged; it can also refer to the pledged word itself. In *The Franklin's Tale* one sign of its centrality as a theme is the way the words *trouthe, trewe, trewely*, echo and re-echo from beginning to end. The suspense generated by the narrative turns on two promises: Dorigen's to Aurelius to be his if he removes the black rocks, and Aurelius's to the Clerk to pay a thousand pounds if he makes it appear that this has been done. In both promises *trouthe* is invoked: Dorigen says,

> Thanne wol I love yow best of any man,
> Have heer my *trouthe*, in al that evere I kan, (325–6)

while Aurelius declares, 'Ye shal be payed *trewely*, by my *trouthe*!' (559). The promises thus given are treated as legally binding contracts, and when, moved by *gentillesse*, Aurelius releases Dorigen and is in turn released by the Clerk, the releases are performed with due formality, in language recalling that actually used in medieval 'quit-claims'. Though only one 'bond' and no written documents are involved, Aurelius nevertheless says to Dorigen:

> I yow relesse, madame, into youre hond
> Quit every serement and every bond

28

> That ye han maad to me as heerbiforn,
> Sith thilke time which that ye were born.   (861–4)

Similarly, the Clerk formally pronounces to Aurelius, 'I release you', and invents a comic version of the intensifying phrase to go with it:

> Sire, I releesse thee thy thousand pound,
> As thou right now were cropen out of the ground . . . (941–2)

The most important invocation of *trouthe*, however, occurs when Arveragus becomes the fourth of the Tale's four central characters to get involved with this theme. Dorigen has promised to love Aurelius if he can perform the task of removing the black rocks. Her belief that this is impossible is underlined: she says so at the time—'For wel I woot that it shal never bitide' (329)—and when it appears to have been done she exclaims in horror, ' . . . wende I nevere by possibilitee / That swich a monstre or merveille mighte be!' (671–2). But that belief, however sincere, does not render the promise invalid. Aurelius announces that the task has been performed, and warns her, 'Aviseth yow er that ye breke youre *trouthe*' (648). She takes the dilemma to her husband, and he tells her that she must keep her promise, because '*Trouthe* is the hyeste thing that man may kepe' (807). Chaucer evidently thought Arveragus's decision might seem strange, for he intervenes to urge us not to jump to premature conclusions:

> Paraventure an heep of yow, ywis,
> Wol holden him a lewed man in this
> That he wol putte his wyf in jupartie.   (821–3)

Yet he also conveys the human drama of the situation. Arveragus's *sententia* does not come out pat, as a complacent pronouncement of general principle. It is the last line of a speech in which he is desperately trying to rouse his wife from her misery, by not letting her see his own agony of mind. But, as he says it, his agony breaks through, and 'with that word he brast anon to wepe' (808). He is stretched on the rack of his own principle and the intensity of the dramatic moment gives the principle itself searing force. Once we begin to take it seriously, though, questions immediately arise. What about Dorigen's original marriage promise to Arveragus, in which *trouthe* was also invoked?

> Sire, I wol be youre humble *trewe* wyf,
> Have heer my *trouthe*, til that myn herte breste.   (86–7)

Trouthe may be 'the hyeste thing that man may kepe' (807), but Arveragus can only make Dorigen keep her *trouthe* to Aurelius by forcing her to break her *trouthe* to himself. Surely her marriage pledge has priority and should invalidate the later promise to Aurelius? Moreover, the medieval understanding was that promises to commit sin were null, and that a married woman could not enter into a contract without her husband's consent (*The Parson's Tale* states that a wife 'hath noon auctoritee to swere ne to bere witnesse withoute leve of hir housbonde, that is hire lord . . .'); these would be further reasons why Dorigen's promise to Aurelius might be considered invalid. Stories perhaps cannot be held to real-life standards of legality, but legal issues often play important roles in medieval romances—indeed, they do so in the discussion of generosity that follows the *Filocolo* story. Since all three of the objections I have listed are mentioned there, Chaucer cannot have been unaware of them. Against the claim that the knight 'used no liberality at all in giving up his wife, because reason dictated that it was proper for him to do so, on account of the oath made by the lady', Fiammetta argues:

> This might be the case indeed, if the oath were valid. But the lady . . . could not make such an oath without the will of her husband; and if she did make it, it was null, because a first oath lawfully made could not reasonably be derogated by any succeeding oath, and especially not by one which was not duly made and for an appropriate cause. It is the custom in matrimonial unions to swear that . . . neither will ever change the one for another. So then, the lady could not make such an oath, and if she did so, . . . she swore an unlawful matter contrary to her first oath. Therefore it could not be binding.

Of course, no such logical analysis occurs in *The Franklin's Tale*; and what follows from all this is not that Chaucer must have expected his readers to supply the arguments he omitted, but that he probably saw *trouthe* in the Tale not as a cut-and-dried issue, but as questionable and apt to arouse further discussion. As with the theme of marriage, so with that of *trouthe*, *The Franklin's Tale* leaves us with uncertainty rather than with the unequivocal doctrine that it may initially appear to offer. In the case of *trouthe*, this is still more so because of the complicated relation of *trouthe* to the theme of *gentillesse*, to which I now turn.

Gentillesse

Gentillesse, gentil and *gentilly* are words used less frequently in *The Franklin's Tale* than *trouthe* and its associated terms. In his Prologue, the Franklin remarks that Breton lays were composed by 'olde *gentil* Britouns' (37), and as the Tale begins Dorigen praises Arveragus's *gentillesse* (82) in not imposing husbandly *maistrie* upon her; but after this the terms disappear until the culminating scenes. Their reappearance may have come as a surprise to

Chaucer's audience, who, not knowing Boccaccio's ver-sions of the story, would have had no reason to expect it to end by taking *gentillesse* as its theme. When Aurelius realizes that he cannot bring himself to demand fulfilment of Dorigen's promise, it is because it would be 'Agains franchise and alle *gentillesse*' (852). He sees Arveragus's determination that Dorigen should keep her *trouthe* as 'grete *gentillesse*' (855), and then releases her from her promise in order to show that a squire can 'doon a *gentil* dede / As wel as kan a knight' (871–2). Aurelius repeats his assessment of Arveragus's *gentillesse* when speaking to the Clerk (923), and the latter in turn sees both husband and lover as having acted *gentilly* and determines to be no less *gentil* himself in forgiving Aurelius his huge debt:

> This philosophre answerde, 'Leeve brother,
> Everich of yow dide *gentilly* til oother.
> Thou art a squier and he is a knight;
> But God forbede, for his blisful might,
> But if a clerk koude doon a *gentil* dede
> As wel as any of yow, it is no drede!' (935–40)

What does *gentillesse* mean? It is usually translated as 'nobility', and *gentil* derives ultimately from the Latin *gentilis*, which meant belonging to the same *gens* (family or race). Originally *gentillesse* referred to high birth; and since in early medieval societies a man's birth normally deter-mined his rank, *gentillesse* was associated with high social rank. The opposite of *gentillesse* was *vileynye* or *cherlissh-nesse*, the state of being a *vileyn* or *cherl* (peasant). Thus *gentil* can refer simply to status, as it probably does when we are told that all the pilgrims admired *The Knight's Tale*, 'And namely the gentils everichon' (And especially each of the *gentil* people). But by Chaucer's time *gentil* and its opposite had come to have moral as well as social significances: *gentillesse* referred to the noble behaviour expected of someone of high birth and rank, *vileynye* or *cherlisshnesse* to the churlish behaviour expected of someone of low birth and rank. Medieval people knew as well as we do, of course, that those of high birth did not always live up to their privileged origins and could behave ignobly, just as those of low birth could behave nobly. But there was always the presumption that birth and conduct would be connected. The connection between social standing and behaviour is made by Chaucer himself in *The Miller's Prologue*, directly after his statement that the *gentils* particularly enjoyed *The Knight's Tale*. He apologizes in advance for any indecency in *The Miller's Tale*: 'The Millere is a cherl, ye knowe wel this,' and therefore, as a matter of course, he will tell 'a cherles tale in his manere'. Here, then, Chaucer is referring *literary* behaviour to social rank; and to modern readers it is striking how deeply medieval conceptions of rank had penetrated even into ideas about literature: both the literary *genres* and their appropriate styles were distinguished on a class basis. It is therefore natural that the Knight and the Squire should tell stories belonging to the genre of chivalric romance, whose characters were *gentil* by birth and behaved in a *gentil* manner, and which were written in the 'high style' taught by textbooks of rhetoric. A connection was to be expected among high birth, moral virtue and elaborate eloquence, and, as we shall see, this underlies the opening of *The Franklin's Prologue*.

We now need to examine more closely the range of meaning covered by *gentillesse* of character and conduct. This is not easily defined, just as in modern English we might find it hard to state the precise meaning of terms such as 'decent' or 'mean' that in practice we use without difficulty to pass judgment on people and behaviour. The criteria employed in everyday life to judge the way people behave and the qualities of character governing their behaviour are largely unspoken and unanalysed, and the same was true in the Middle Ages. In the best attempt to analyse *gentillesse*[1] the following are listed as the inner qualities consistently associated with it: *trouthe* (in its general sense as loyalty and faithfulness); compassion (including not just sympathy for others but willingness to help them); graciousness or gentleness; generosity or liberality; cheerfulness; concern for reputation; moderation or patience; and the capacity for romantic love. Some of these we have already encountered in our examination of *The Franklin's Tale*; nearly all do in fact characterize its characters' behaviour, and the wide range of qualities included within *gentillesse* may be one reason why *gentillesse* itself can remain unmentioned between the Tale's beginning and its end—the characters are behaving *gentilly* even while displaying many other virtues. We have seen something of the importance of *trouthe*, compassion and patience in the Tale, and the competition in generosity in which the three men display their *gentillesse* is the goal of the whole narrative. Romantic love obviously plays a crucial part in Arveragus's wooing of Dorigen, her misery during his absence, and Aurelius's indirect attempts to attract her with love-songs and looks, his love-sickness when unsuccessful, and his willingness to spend more than he has to perform the impossible task she sets him. Romantic love is at the

[1] Lindsay A. Mann, '"Gentilesse" and the Franklin's Tale', *Studies in Philology*, 63 (1966).

centre of all three characters' lives; and they feel love so strongly that the cheerfulness expected of the *gentil* lover is the one *gentil* quality their behaviour generally lacks. Graciousness is a marked feature of Arveragus's treatment of his wife when she admits her promise to Aurelius: he responds 'with glad chiere, in freendly wise . . .' (795), and attempts to behave cheerfully as well as in a kindly manner, but his suffering is such that he cannot avoid tears.

The one aspect of *gentillesse* that may need further explanation is concern for reputation, shown in the pursuit of *worship*, *name* or honour, and the avoidance of shame. At various times this concern motivates Arveragus, Dorigen and Aurelius. Arveragus leaves Dorigen for two years to 'seke in armes *worshipe* and *honour*' (139), having previously insisted on concealing his renunciation of *maistrie* over her, because 'the *name* of soverainetee, / That wolde he have for *shame* of his degree' (79–80). The last phrase could mean 'out of regard for his rank' (as a husband or a knight), or possibly 'because he was ashamed of his rank'—that is, being of lower rank than his well-connected wife (63), he feared the damage to his reputation if people knew that he did not exercise husbandly mastery over her. In any event, he is concerned with his standing in others' eyes. Later, having exercised that mastery by instructing Dorigen to keep her promise to Aurelius, Arveragus insists that she must conceal the consequences:

> I yow forbede, up peyne of deeth,
> That nevere, whil thee lasteth lyf ne breeth,
> To no wight telle thou of this aventure—
> As I may best, I wol my wo endure—
> Ne make no contenance of hevinesse,
> That folk of yow may demen harm or gesse.   (809–14)

Dorigen's distress at the thought of becoming Aurelius's mistress is expressed in terms not of physical revulsion but of concern for her honour: if a knight's reputation depends on martial deeds, a lady's depends on chastity or married fidelity. She too speaks of shame, honour's opposite:

> But nathelees, yet have I levere to lese
> My lyf than of my body to have a *shame*,
> Or knowe myselven fals, or lese my *name* . . . (688–90)

Concern for what others think of her ('lese my name') is set alongside self-knowledge ('knowe myselven fals'). Finally, Aurelius shows his concern with reputation when the moment comes to pay the Clerk his fee. He knows that he has nothing like the necessary sum, so he will have to sell his inheritance, reducing himself to beggary, and then leave Brittany because 'heere may I nat dwelle, / And *shamen* al my kinrede in this place' (892–3).

The characters' pervasive anxiety to avoid shame has often been regarded as a weakness. It appears most strongly in Arveragus, and he has been accused of callousness in abandoning his wife to gain military glory abroad, and of revealing not just a craven obsession with 'what the neighbours think' but monstrous selfishness in seeing Dorigen's violation by Aurelius as a matter of damage to *his* reputation— 'As *I* may best, *I* wol *my* wo endure'. Yet Arveragus, 'of chivalrie the flour, . . . the worthy man of armes' (416, 420), is wholeheartedly admired within the Tale; and, tempting though the unfavourable view may be, it is probably mistaken. The concern for gaining and keeping honour and avoiding shame is part of a medieval conception of *gentillesse* that Chaucer shared. He was aware that this concern could be exaggerated, and he doubtless considered people's sense of inner worth even more important than their sense of what others thought of them, but I do not believe he thought the latter unimportant or unworthy. And, though our culture sees sincerity as the criterion of moral value, to the exclusion of social pressures, perhaps we should consider that the two may be less opposed than they seem. For most of us, in reality if not in theory, our sense of our own moral status is strongly dependent on our sense of how others regard us. Our vision of the right way to live, or of the right thing to do in particular circumstances, does not come to us directly from God or conscience, but is mediated by internalized images of ourselves as judged by other human beings. The very terms we use to assess conduct (right, decent, mean, rotten, and so on) belong to languages we did not invent for ourselves, and their meanings are given by the communities to which we belong. In this respect, we differ little from Chaucer and his contemporaries; but we may be less willing than they to admit how much our moral sense and conduct depend on images of how others see us.

To return to *gentillesse*, we have seen that in medieval thought it was closely connected with social rank. Chaucer, however, was concerned with the possibility of breaking this tie. In the *Filocolo* the competition in generosity among the three men is not framed in terms of rank. Tebano's extreme poverty is emphasized, but Tarolfo and the husband are both knights, and neither Tarolfo nor Tebano mentions anything but generosity itself (*liberalità*) as motivation in relinquishing the fulfilment of the promises made. In *The Franklin's Tale* the structure of rank and the argument are quite different. Arveragus is a knight, Aurelius a squire, and the Clerk a prosperous professional man, not noticeably poorer than they and even having a household squire of his own, but lacking their social status; and the last two insist that their acts of *gentillesse* are intended to prove that moral conduct is not restricted by social position. A squire is eager to show that he can 'doon a gentil dede / As wel as kan a knight' (871–2), and a clerk, contemplating the *gentil* acts of 'a squier and . . . a knight' (937), thinks it would be shameful 'But if a clerk koude doon a gentil dede / As wel as any of yow' (939–40). In *The Wife of Bath's Tale* and elsewhere Chaucer presents the same argument, emphasizing that virtue differs from birth and that moral values are superior to social values. This was by no means a revolutionary view: he could have encountered it in Juvenal, in Boethius, in Jean de Meun and in Dante. In the *Consolation*, for example, Boethius argues that

> yif thou ne have no gentilesse of thiself (*that is to seyn, prys that cometh of thy deserte*), foreyne gentilesse ne maketh the nat gentil. But certes yif ther be ony good in gentilesse, I trowe it be al only this, that it semeth as that a maner necessité be imposed to gentil men for that thei ne schulde nat owtrayen or forlynen fro the vertus of hir noble kynrede.[1]

Jean de Meun, offering a similar argument, adds that clerks—men of learning— ' have a greater opportunity than have princes or kings, who know nothing of what is written, to be noble, courteous and wise'. This would have a special bearing on the Clerk of Orleans, and indeed on Chaucer himself, for he too was a clerk. There is every reason to suppose that this argument represented what Chaucer truly believed, and as a successful clerk (a civil

[1] Chaucer's translation, Book III, prosa 6, with his explanatory gloss in brakcets: 'if you have no *gentillesse* of your own (that is, reputation you have earned for yourself), others' *gentillesse* cannot make you *gentil*. But truly if there is any good in *gentillesse*, I believe it is only that it seems as though a kind of obligation is imposed on *gentil* men not to stray or degenerate from the virtues of their noble relations.'

servant and a diplomat as well as a learned poet), born into a wealthy bourgeois family, whose life brought him into constant contact with those of *gentil* birth, most of them less gifted than himself, he had every reason to believe it.

Gentillesse in *The Franklin's Tale*, then, is an ethical quality that bears no necessary relation to high birth; the knight may set the standard of *gentil* conduct, but the squire and the clerk can match him. The question remains, what relation exists between the two themes of *gentillesse* and *trouthe*? We have seen that *trouthe* is one of the qualities understood to make up *gentillesse*, yet it would appear that in the Tale *gentillesse* involves abandoning *trouthe*. *Trouthe* sticks to the letter of promises, but *gentillesse* seems to demand the very opposite. To understand the underlying thought, we must put both virtues in a different context. The Tale's characters are pagans, and a common medieval term either for pagans or for all nations other than the Jews is 'gentiles'. Orthodox religious thought saw God as having originally made a covenant with the Jews as his chosen people, which they interpreted as involving no more and no less than an exact adherence to the laws revealed to them by Jehovah. In due course, God sent his Son to fulfil this 'old covenant' and to establish a new and better covenant, based on a redeeming love that went beyond mere law. But the Jews, refusing to recognize Jesus as their Messiah, rejected the new covenant, and God then deprived them of their status as his chosen people, and instead offered salvation to the gentiles. Thus the Jews became thralls (a theory that ratified their actual situation in medieval Europe, persecuted, often exiled, and forbidden to own land) while the gentiles became *gentil*—a pun found in many texts right down to Shakespeare's *Merchant of Venice*. In *Piers Plowman*, one of the most widely read English poems of the time, Chaucer's contemporary William Langland described this transformation as follows: Jesus came to earth as a conqueror

> To make lordes of laddes, of lond that he wynneth,
> And fre men foule thralles, that folwen noght his lawes.
> The Jewes, that were gentil men, Jesu thei despised—
> Bothe his loore and his lawe; now are thei lowe cherles.
> As wide as the world is, wonyeth ther noon
> But under tribut and taillage as tikes and cherles;
> And tho that bicome Cristene bi counseil of the Baptiste
> Aren frankeleyns, free men thorugh fullynge that thei toke
> And gentil men with Jesu . . .[1]

Thought along these lines may lie behind the movement from *trouthe* to *gentillesse* in *The Franklin's Tale*. Arveragus and Dorigen are noble pagans, *gentil* gentiles, who long for freedom in their relations, for

> Love is a thing as any spirit free.
> Wommen, of kinde, desiren libertee,
> And nat to been constreyned as a thral;
> And so doon men, if I sooth seyen shal.   (95–8)

The means they choose to gain liberty are based on *trouthe*, on binding promises, freely undertaken (Arveragus swore 'Of his free wil' (73) not to impose *maistrie* upon Dorigen) but leading to the bondage of a covenant understood as a legal contract. Medieval readers might have seen them as analogous to the Jews before Christ's coming, seeking

---

[1] *The Vision of Piers Plowman*, ed. A. V. C. Schmidt (Dent, 1978), B.XIX. 32–40: 'to make commoners into lords, from the land that he gains, and free men who do not follow his laws into vile slaves. The Jews, who were *gentil* men, despised Jesus, both his teaching and his law; now they are base serfs. None of them dwells throughout the world except under tribute and taxation, as dogs and peasants; and those who followed John the Baptist's advice and became Christians are now franklins, made into free men and *gentil* men with Jesus by the baptism they accepted . . .'.

spiritual liberation by the best means open to them, the covenant with Jehovah. The consequence of this reliance on *trouthe* emerges at one of the Tale's most painful moments, when Arveragus feels obliged to tell his wife to keep her promise to Aurelius, for

> 'Trouthe is the hyeste thing that man may kepe'—
> But with that word he brast anon to wepe.   (807–8)

This absolute adherence to *trouthe* is rightly seen as admirable by Aurelius, just as Aurelius's equally absolute adherence to *trouthe*—'I failled nevere of my trouthe as yit' (905)—is rightly seen as admirable by the Clerk. But *trouthe* alone cannot make gentiles into 'free men . . . And gentil men'. True freedom is gained by going beyond *trouthe*, not keeping rigidly to covenants but freely dissolving them, as when Aurelius releases Dorigen from her promise as completely as if she were an innocent child—

> I yow relesse, madame, into youre hond
> Quit every serement and every bond
> That ye han maad to me as heerbiforn,
> Sith thilke time which that ye were born   (861–4)

—and the Clerk releases Aurelius equally completely from his. The word *free* in Chaucer's English means 'generous' as well as 'free'; and *frely* has both senses when Aurelius explains to the Clerk how his treatment of Dorigen matched her husband's:

> And right as *frely* as he sente hire me,
> As *frely* sente I hire to him ageyn.   (932–3)

The noun corresponding to *fre* is *franchise*, which similarly means both generosity and liberty; what persuades Aurelius to release Dorigen from her promise is his recognition that to make her keep it would be 'Agains *franchise* and alle gentillesse' (852). Thus a story that begins with a quest for freedom in the sense of liberty ends with a competition in freedom in the sense of generosity. Given that Langland speaks of the gentiles becoming 'frankeleyns, free men', it seems unlikely to be by accident that this story is told by a Franklin. But it is important to grasp that the Tale's movement from *trouthe* to *gentillesse* or *franchise* does not involve cancelling out *trouthe*. Aurelius invokes his *trouthe* (865) even as he swears never to reproach Dorigen with the promise from which he has released her, and we are assured that Dorigen was 'trewe for everemoore' to Arveragus (883) after they were set free from their dilemma. The New Law of Christianity did not destroy the Old Law based on the covenant between the Jews and Jehovah but fulfilled it; similarly, in one critic's words,

> in the poem the Christian virtue of *freedom* (generosity) fulfills the Old Testament contractual law of *trouthe* (the covenant). Both virtues are important, since *trouthe* calls *freedom* into existence as the Old Testament may be said to have called into existence the New.

Or, as another remarks, the story reveals 'that absolute adherence to *biheste* [promise] may, against all the odds, lead to freedom from its narrow constraints'.[1]

If this is really what *The Franklin's Tale* reveals, it can help us to understand why Chaucer, having changed the task imposed by the wife in Boccaccio's versions, nevertheless retained the midwinter setting belonging to the

[1] E. T. Donaldson (ed.), *Chaucer's Poetry: An Anthology for the Modern Reader*, 2nd edn (Ronald Press, 1975); John M. Fyler, 'Love and Degree in the *Franklin's Tale*', *Chaucer Review*, 21 (1986–7).

original task. Aurelius and the Clerk leave Orleans for Brittany,

> And this was, as thise bookes me remembre,
> The colde, frosty seson of Decembre.   (571-2)

There follows a passage brilliantly evoking that season in terms that are at once mythological, astronomical and meteorological:

> Phebus wax old, and hewed lyk laton,
> That in his hoote declinacion
> Shoon as the burned gold with stremes brighte;
> But now in Capricorn adoun he lighte,
> Where as he shoon ful pale, I dar wel seyn.
> The bittre frostes, with the sleet and reyn,
> Destroyed hath the grene in every yerd.
> Janus sit by the fyr, with double berd,
> And drinketh of his bugle horn the wyn;
> Biforn him stant brawen of the tusked swyn,
> And 'Nowel' crieth every lusty man.   (573-83)

Descriptions of winter are rare in medieval English narratives, and nowhere else in Chaucer is there one remotely comparable to this. The zodiacal detail is compatible with the pagan setting of the whole story, 'Phebus' being the same as the sun-god to whom Aurelius had prayed earlier; Janus too belongs to pagan mythology, as god of beginnings. But 'Nowel' is a Christian slogan, alluding specifically to Christmas, the birth of Christ. We seem to get a glimpse of Christian truth emerging amid the rituals that 'hethen folk useden in thilke dayes' (621). It is an appropriate setting for the movement from the Old Law to the New that can be shadowily discerned in the story of *The Franklin's Tale*.

THE TALE AND ITS CHARACTERS

Much of what remains to be discussed can most conveniently be related to the Tale's characters, and especially to Aurelius, Dorigen and the Clerk. Arveragus is less in need of further discussion: it is in him that the explicit themes focus, yet he is off-stage for most of the important events, and changes little as the Tale proceeds. He is the very embodiment of *trouthe*, which by its nature is unchanging, and though he is the means by which 'absolute adherence to *biheste*' is able to 'lead to freedom from its narrow constraints', he himself arrives at no new understanding. Chaucer's farewell to him is appropriately brief: Dorigen tells him about her final meeting with Aurelius,

> And be ye siker, he was so weel apayd
> That it were inpossible me to write.
> What sholde I lenger of this cas endite? (876–8)

Of the others, I begin with Aurelius, because he illustrates most clearly the conventionality in terms of which the story is initially framed. When the characters enter, they interest us not as persons but as units in a familiar pattern, symbolic of general feelings and ideas, and far distant from the complexities of our individual lives; yet as the Tale proceeds, this conventionality is deployed and modified in ways that evoke something more inward and perhaps more individual.

Aurelius: Convention and Inner Life

Aurelius is first seen dancing among Dorigen's friends, who are trying to comfort her in her husband's absence. He is described in a leisurely manner and in superlative terms, as 'a squier',

> That fressher was and jolier of array,
> As to my doom, than is the month of May.
> He singeth, daunceth, passinge any man
> That is, or was, sith that the world bigan.
> Therwith he was, if men sholde him discrive,
> Oon of the beste faringe man on live;
> Yong, strong, right vertuous, and riche, and wys,
> And wel biloved, and holden in greet prys.   (255–62)

Despite the personal touches in the narration—'As to my doom . . . if men sholde him discrive'—the aim is not to individualize Aurelius but to classify him: he is everything a young courtier ought to be. The comparison to 'the month of May', making him symbolize the season of youth and love, has also appeared in the portrait of the pilgrim-Squire in *The General Prologue*—'He was as fressh as is the month of May'—and the general similarity of the descriptions indicates how little the two squires are individualized. It is in accordance with literary convention that Aurelius should fall in love with Dorigen, and that his love should be of the extremest possible kind. In medieval courtly literature, the unaccepted lover's mental state is always one of intense misery. This suffering was sketched in the case of Arveragus before Dorigen accepted him; now, in Aurelius's case, it is developed more fully. He dares not speak to Dorigen, and can only disclose his love obliquely, 'as in a general compleyning' (273). He falls into despair and 'langwissheth as a furye dooth in helle' (278). At last he nerves himself to declare his love, with the unhappy result we have seen. Now his *penaunce* is redoubled. He feels death approaching: 'Him semed that he felte his herte colde' (351). He becomes delirious, and makes an insane prayer to Apollo, begging him to request his sister, Lucina the moon-goddess, to cause an unusually high spring tide to cover the rocks, and by retarding her rotation about the earth to make it remain for two years. We are told that he prayed 'in his raving' (354) and that 'he Niste what he spak' (356), yet—and this is typical of medieval poetry—Chaucer makes no attempt to introduce signs of delirium into the speech's manner. It is long and carefully constructed, lucid in argument and elaborate in syntax, stating exactly the mythological and scientific basis for his request. It is evidently more important that the speech should be a clearly reasoned *pleynt* than that Aurelius's *raving* should be realistically imitated. His science is mistaken, according to Chaucer's geocentric medieval cosmology, because even if Lucina did perform the *miracle* of circling the earth at the same rate as the sun this would not keep the high tide in being. We are doubtless expected to recognize this: Aurelius's delirium appears in the irrationality of his object, and that will be apparent only if lucidly expounded.

Aurelius prays for 49 lines, and then swoons, 'And longe time he lay forth in a traunce' (409). Now comes a further description of his misery, still in terms of courtly convention. Passionate love was literally regarded as a disease, referred to in *The Knight's Tale* as 'Hereos, the loveris maladye', and regarded seriously enough to be discussed in medical treatises; its symptoms were those of a prolonged bout of influenza. And, given the association in medieval culture of rationality and activity with men and of emotionalism and helplessness with women, 'the loveris maladye' involves a kind of feminization of the male lover—hence Aurelius's identification with Echo (279–80). He takes to his bed, and for 'Two yeer and moore' (430) is unable to walk. He tells no one but his brother of the cause of his illness, and his brother sees only that he must be 'warisshed' (466: cured). The only cure is to obtain Dorigen's love, and so the magician is brought in. Yet even Aurelius is not presented solely in conventional terms. In all the swooning, sickness and singing of 'layes, / Songes, compleintes, roundels, virelayes' (275–6), there has been one striking human touch to add conviction to the traditional account of the lover's sufferings. It is presented as an exception: he dares disclose nothing to Dorigen,

> Save that, paraventure, somtime at daunces,
> Ther yonge folk kepen hir observaunces,
> It may wel be he looked on hir face
> In swich a wise as man that asketh grace;
> But nothing wiste she of his entente.   (283–7)

This mute look, lost in the bustle of the dance and not understood, mentioned with a hesitance ('It may wel be . . .') that evokes his own, brings the convention to life.

The scenes in which Aurelius and Dorigen are together illustrate especially well Chaucer's skill in modifying the conventional with touches of inwardness. Aurelius's declaration of love is a formal speech full of the jargon of service, pity, pain and death, and rhetorically organized with great lucidity. Dorigen's reaction is quite different, unpredictable and lifelike:

> She gan to looke upon Aurelius:
> 'Is this youre wil,' quod she, 'and sey ye thus?
> Nevere erst,' quod she, 'ne wiste I what ye mente'.   (307–9)

There is a pause as she stares at him, taking in what he has said, and seeming to see him for the first time; then she stammers out her reply, the stammer being suggested by the way 'quod she' twice interrupts her in mid-sentence. She goes on to give a downright refusal, only to qualify it with the ill-considered condition. She will become his mistress after all—*if* he can remove the rocks from the coast of Brittany. Taking her seriously, he asks in anguish, 'Is ther noon oother grace in yow?' (327). Her reply is again downright and unashamedly innocent, with its question that strikes at the root of courtly conventions:

> Lat swiche folies out of youre herte slide.
> What deyntee sholde a man han in his lyf
> For to go love another mannes wyf,
> That hath hir body whan so that him liketh? (330–3)

He turns away with a melodramatic threat of death, and immediately her other friends appear, knowing nothing of the drama that has just been played out, and ready to begin some new entertainment. Chaucer imagined the episode entirely in terms of speech and gesture, yet so vividly as to evoke the consciousnesses of the characters as they first become aware of each other's true natures.

A second point in the treatment of Aurelius where the conventional is given new life is the scene revealing the consequences of the Clerk's apparent success in making the rocks vanish. Having thanked first him and then Venus, Aurelius goes to a temple where he expects to find Dorigen. The speech in which he tells her what has happened (639–66) begins as a formal *pleynt*, like his earlier prayer to Apollo, and with a similarly composed and logical syntax, seeming to belie his emotion:

> 'My righte lady,' quod this woful man,
> 'Whom I moost drede and love as I best kan,
> And lothest were of al this world displese,
> Nere it that I for yow have swich disese
> That I moste dien heere at youre foot anon,
> Noght wolde I telle how me is wo bigon'. (639–44)

Once more he is using the conventional jargon of *fine amour*, now as a barrier against his own feelings: at once embarrassed and wildly excited, he is evading the point he really wants to make. Gradually, however, emotion breaks through the lucid rhetorical structure, and he loses himself in parentheses that are intended to reassure but are in fact merely confusing:

> For, madame, wel ye woot what ye han hight—
> Nat that I chalange any thing of right
> Of yow, my soverein lady, but youre grace—
> But in a gardyn yond, at swich a place,
> Ye woot right wel what ye bihighten me . . .   (651–5)

He cannot bring himself to say directly either what she promised or what he has done, and it is not till the last line of the whole speech that he mentions the crucial word 'rokkes'. In this Chaucerian blend of convention and realism, the conventional is as necessary as its opposite, for it needs to exist in order to be so convincingly broken down.

In this and earlier scenes Aurelius's inner life has been conveyed largely by outer means, through speech and its bodily accompaniments. This is normal in medieval English romances; but when Aurelius moves from *trouthe* to *franchise* Chaucer does something less common, representing this turning-point as an inner process preceding speech. After he has met Dorigen and learned that, under her husband's instructions, she is coming to keep her promise,

> Aurelius gan wondren on this cas,
> And in his herte hadde greet compassioun
> Of hire and of hire lamentacioun,
> And of Arveragus, the worthy knight,
> That bad hire holden al that she had hight
> So looth him was his wyf sholde breke hir trouthe;
> And in his herte he caughte of this greet routhe,

> Consideringe the beste on every side,
> That fro his lust yet were him levere abide
> Than doon so heigh a cherlissh wrecchednesse
> Agains franchise and alle gentillesse;
> For which in fewe wordes seyde he thus . . .　　(842–53)

All this happens 'Amidde the toun, right in the quikkest strete' (830), yet inwardly, 'in his herte' (843, 848)—the weighing of different aspects of the situation (including the inner lives of other characters), the recategorization of his intended response as 'cherlissh wrecchednesse', and finally the realization that his self-image prevents him from acting against *franchise* and *gentillesse*. It is a moment of self-recognition and existential choice that nevertheless grows out of the communal values of his and Chaucer's society, those of 'the quikkest strete'. The character who began by seeming the most conventional of all, just a generic young squire, has acquired a complex inner life in which terms that originally had a public, social meaning and relationship take on a new configuration and a fuller, more subjective reality.

Dorigen: Feeling, Landscape and the Role of Women

We have seen that in this tale of powerful feelings Dorigen's feelings are at the centre. Her overwhelming grief at Arveragus's absence leads to the first of her two major speeches, the one reproaching God for having created the black rocks. In the poems that Chaucer set in pagan antiquity, characters in distress typically generalize their situations and ask not just, 'Why has this happened to me?' but, 'Why is the world so organized that things like this can happen to anyone?' The thought involved in such philosophical questionings, as we have seen, is taken from

Boethius's *Consolation*, and this is what happens with Dorigen. After Arveragus has gone, she walks on the sea-shore 'Hire to disporte' (177); but she regrets that none of the ships she sees is bringing her husband back, and then her attention turns to 'thise rokkes blake' (219), and these fill her with fear. Her thoughts and feelings are represented in a passionate speech arraigning the divine ordering of the universe. Much of its phrasing recalls Chaucer's translation of Boethius, and in particular a speech in which Boethius, in his dialogue with Philosophy, asks why God, who orders the non-human world with such regularity, leaves human life to the disorderly and arbitrary government of Fortune. In the *Consolation*, however, there are no black rocks to form an anomaly in the non-human world as well. These are the imaginative centre of Dorigen's speech, a concrete instance challenging the generalizations of philosophy. The speech's philosophical content is marshalled as an argument addressed to God—one side of an imaginary disputation in which the other party remains silent—but it is also presented so as to express intense feeling. The bland confidence and rhetorical high style of Dorigen's first sentence—

> Eterne God, that thurgh thy purveiaunce
> Ledest the world by certein governaunce,
> In idel, as men seyn, ye no thing make   (193–5)

—are interrupted by the eager familiarity of her second, where the rocks themselves, surrounded by emotive epithets, elbow aside the normal syntactical structure, so that the first four lines define the object of a verb for which room cannot be found until the fifth:

> But, Lord, thise grisly feendly rokkes blake,
> That semen rather a foul confusion
> Of werk than any fair creacion
> Of swich a parfit wys God and a stable,
> Why han ye wroght this werk unresonable?   (196–200)

And the delay gives special emphasis to 'Why . . .?'. Dorigen, full of the horror aroused by seeing the rocks, abruptly takes God to task, and cannot leave him alone, though she turns briefly aside once to conduct a contemptuous argument with his professional defenders, the 'clerkes'. Again and again she reverts to the rocks themselves, the one horrifyingly undeniable fact in a dubious metaphysical situation.

This speech closely resembles one in *The Knight's Tale* in which Palamon asks what the gods care for men. In both cases, arguments borrowed from the *Consolation*, and there used *against* Philosophy, are presented with passionate conviction and concrete illustration, while Philosophy's answers are omitted. In *The Knight's Tale* it is pagan gods who are arraigned, but in *The Franklin's Tale*, despite the pagan setting, the God addressed differs little from the Christian God. He is a perfect, eternal and immutable creator, who has made man in his own image, and whose ways are justified by 'clerkes'; and the speech's terminology is that of medieval Christian scholasticism—*purveiaunce, argumentz, causes, conclusion, disputison*. The speech is disturbing, and, as the poem's focus moves from metaphysics to ethics, it cannot be said that its questions are ever answered. It no more represents Chaucer's considered view of the universe than Macbeth's 'Tomorrow, and tomorrow, and tomorrow' represents Shakespeare's; but Dorigen's passionate questionings have engaged the poet's feelings and imagination at a deep level.

In this speech the black rocks, under the influence of Dorigen's 'derke fantasye' (172), have become a symbol of some flaw in the divinely ordered course of nature. To grasp their symbolism, we need to set them alongside the Tale's other antithetical symbolic landscape, the garden. With striking dramatic contrast, this is described immediately after Dorigen's 'black rocks' speech. Her friends persuade her to stop brooding over the rocks and join them on a picnic. We follow them, and the springtime garden now described belongs to a widespread convention in medieval literature also found in garden descriptions in *The Knight's Tale* and *The Merchant's Tale*. It originates in the pastoral literature of antiquity and in descriptions of the garden of Eden in Genesis, of the 'garden enclosed' in the Song of Songs (or Song of Solomon), and of the heavenly Jerusalem in the Apocalypse (or Book of Revelation). It has paradisal qualities, is often associated with the female body, and may be, as in *The Franklin's Tale*, a place of temptation. Under the influence of the *Roman de la Rose*, this Maytime garden had become the traditional setting for love adventures. The description is symbolic rather than realistic, though real medieval gardens also followed the pattern of the literary convention. The garden of love in Guillaume de Lorris's first part of the *Roman de la Rose* was described as a kind of secular paradise inhabited by the god of love. The same paradisal comparison appears in *The Franklin's Tale*, but with a special emphasis on the human artifice involved in constructing it:

> And craft of mannes hand so curiously
> Arrayed hadde this gardyn, trewely,
> That nevere was ther gardyn of swich prys,
> But if it were the verray paradis.   (237–40)

This stress on artifice, also found in the statement that May had 'peynted' it (235) with leaves and flowers, sets the garden in opposition to the rocks.

It is not uncommon for contrasting settings to contribute to the meaning of medieval narratives. In *Sir Gawain and the Green Knight*, comfortable castles are set against exposed wintry landscapes; in *The Knight's Tale*, a prison and a garden, surrounded by the same wall, stand as images of opposing aspects of civilization—constraint and protection. In *The Franklin's Tale*, the garden is 'ther biside' (230) the cliffs from which the black rocks can be seen, the one made by human beings, the other by God—realms of artifice and of nature. The meanings of these two settings shift in relation to events. In May the garden offers comfort in Dorigen's misery, a human refuge against obsessive thoughts of nature's harshness; but it is also the place where, even as she rejects Aurelius's attempted seduction, she makes the 'rash promise' that almost leads her to disaster. It appears that the garden, ruined by winter, is to be the scene of her violation, yet ultimately her encounter with Aurelius on the way there, 'of aventure or grace' (836), produces the change of heart in him that obviates the final garden scene we have been expecting. There is no tradition of rock settings in medieval poetry as there is of garden settings, and these rocks vary in meaning still more widely than the garden. As we have seen, they are a real geographical feature, but their significance lies not in their mere genuineness, but in the imaginative force they acquire from the play of Dorigen's emotions on them: they are transformed into symbols by Dorigen herself. First she sees only the danger they present to her husband's safe return, and they signify the 'foul confusion' (197) of the created world, its irrational enmity towards human happiness. But once they seem to have disappeared, her happiness turns out to have depended on their existence, and they come to symbolize the rational order of nature on which she has always relied:

> For wende I nevere by possibilitee
> That swich a monstre or merveille mighte be!
> It is agains the proces of nature. (671–3)

The rocks' very materiality, their existence outside human understanding and poetic convention, frees them to bear whatever meaning our imaginations may impose. One recent critic sees them as a 'reification of ... Dorigen's hostility towards her husband' for his absence; another remarks that 'to the lover the rocks are the excluding barrier of Dorigen's married state'; a third suggests that 'The marriage ... has been a too balanced partnership, suppressing ... the raggedness of boundaries between two selves whose bodies are each other's rocky coasts'.[1] Probably none of those ideas had occurred to Chaucer, but stories often mean more than their tellers know, and, as responses to the relation between the rocks and the marriage, these are legitimate and thought-provoking.

Dorigen's second major speech, comprising over 11 per cent of the Tale, is her *compleynt* addressed to Fortune, listing twenty-two examples of ladies who died rather than suffer dishonour. What to make of this has been a major

[1] Linda Charnes, '"This Werk Unresonable": Narrative Frustration and Generic Redistribution in Chaucer's *Franklin's Tale*', *Chaucer Review*, 23 (1988–9); W. A. Davenport, *Chaucer: Complaint and Narrative* (D. S. Brewer, 1988); Ellen E. Martin, 'The Romance of Anxiety in Chaucer's *Franklin's Tale*', in *Voices in Translation: The Authority of "Olde Bookes" in Medieval Literature*, ed. Deborah M. Sinnreich-Levi and Gale Sigal (AMS Press, 1992).

problem for readers. It is clearly designed as a rhetorical set-piece, a formal lament marked as such by its framing lines, 'In hire *compleynt*, as ye shal after heere' (682) and 'Thus *pleyned* Dorigen a day or tweye . . .' (785). On a first reading, we can see its appropriateness to its context. The apparently impossible has apparently occurred, and Dorigen sees no way but suicide of avoiding irremediable shame. She is a pagan (thus Christian repentance is never a possibility), and suicide was regarded by pagans as a noble way of escaping humiliation; her examples of women who killed themselves to avoid dishonour all concern pagans. Both the formal *compleynt* and the catalogue of *exempla* (stories from real life chosen to illustrate some general principle) are traditional devices belonging to the high style of medieval rhetoric; they may have less appeal for us than for medieval readers, we may feel that Chaucer has miscalculated in allowing Dorigen to speak at such length, but that should not alter our assessment of his intention. Closer examination, though, suggests a different interpretation. All the *exempla* come from a single source, Saint Jerome's *Adversus Jovinianum*, a major source of medieval writings in favour of virginity and against marriage. But their order in Jerome is different from that in Chaucer, and Chaucer's order suggests that he went through Jerome's treatise at least twice. The first time he selected *exempla* carefully, classified them (723–6), told them at length, and then came to what seems intended as a conclusion (747–53). The second time, determined to lengthen the original list, he made use of all conceivably relevant material, and told the stories only briefly or allusively. This evidence indicates that the speech's length was calculated, and may indeed have been its chief purpose. Dorigen uses the *exempla* to prove to herself that her only escape is suicide, but in the end, after 'a day or tweye, / Purposinge evere that she wolde deye' (785–6), she does not die but confesses to her husband and leaves it to him to decide the outcome. In the course of the speech we watch her struggling in vain to take the heroic resolution she believes to be right. She begins with an *exemplum* laden with expressions of exaggerated horror—'ful of cursednesse . . . in despit . . . God yeve hem meschaunce!' (696–702)—and culminating in the wonderfully implausible picture of a band of virgins jumping *secretly* into a well to drown themselves. The succeeding *exempla*, growing shorter and less pertinent as her desperation increases, serve as a way not of nerving herself to act, but of delaying till Arveragus returns. They include references to one lady who killed herself not to avoid dishonour but through anxiety about her absent husband (a situation closer to Dorigen's than she may realize), and to another who built her husband a splendid tomb after his death—a situation spectacularly irrelevant to her own! The list concludes with three names included with total disregard for relevance, those of a lady who refused to marry a second time, one who killed her nurse for trying to persuade her to marry a second time, and one who showed her *parfit wyfhod* by putting up with her husband's bad breath—'She said, "I thought the mouths of all men smelled like that",' Jerome explains. Chaucer is unlikely to have had readers able to identify Bilyea, Rodogone and Valeria, and we may suspect a private joke; but the very length of the list produces an effect of bathos, as Dorigen falls short of the heroism she so vividly imagines, and uses words as a way of *not* dealing with her real situation. Yet we surely cannot wish her to kill herself, and the outcome of the delay is an ending happier for all the characters than we could have predicted.

Throughout the Tale, Dorigen's capacity for feeling is accompanied by the habit of over-dramatizing her feelings—a characteristic noted quite early in the dry comment that her demonstrative grief at Arveragus's absence showed her behaving 'As doon thise noble wives whan hem liketh' (146). To arrive at a comprehensive judgment on her behaviour is not easy, and is probably not meant to be. Some readers have thought a derogatory response appropriate not just to her self-dramatizing tendencies but to what they see as the blatantly erroneous theology of her black rocks speech; others have felt nothing but sympathy and admiration. Cultural changes produce different readings, and in recent years the growing influence of feminism has been especially fruitful in stimulating new views of Dorigen and her role in the Tale. It might once have seemed obvious that Arveragus's insistence on *trouthe* was simply admirable and Dorigen's promise to Aurelius simply rash, and that the only question raised was that explicitly asked at the Tale's conclusion. More recent readings have noted that *The Franklin's Tale* is a man's story about a competition in *gentillesse* among three men, in which the only woman features as little more than a commodity. Without Dorigen there would be no story, yet her own husband explicitly and harshly forbids her to tell the story as hers:

> I yow forbede, up peyne of deeth,
> That nevere, whil thee lasteth lyf ne breeth,
> To no wight telle thou of this aventure . . .   (809–11)

Introduction

The Wife of Bath shrewdly observes in her Prologue that the reason for the antifeminist bias of 'official' medieval culture is that the histories are all written by men (and celibate priests at that):

> By God, if wommen hadde writen stories,
> As clerkes han withinne hire oratories,
> They wolde han writen of men moore wikkednesse
> Than al the mark of Adam may redresse.

(By God, if women had written histories, as clerks have in their ivory towers, they would have written more evil of men than the whole male sex could make good.) A version of *The Franklin's Tale* told by Dorigen, or by any woman, might sound very different from the version we have. As it is, in the interest of demonstrating male generosity, Dorigen is dispatched like an uncomprehending parcel from one man to another—

> And right as frely as he sente hire me,
> As frely sente I hire to him ageyn   (932–3)

—and her role as an object of exchange is highlighted by the fact that in these male transactions her counterpart is a large sum of money. The Tale's setting is unquestionably patriarchal, one in which the truth about marriage is that stated bluntly by Dorigen herself:

> What deyntee sholde a man han in his lyf
> For to go love another mannes wyf,
> *That hath hir body whan so that him liketh?*   (331–3)

There is no question of a woman having her husband's body 'whan so that hir liketh'—that is the cause of Dorigen's grief at Arveragus's absence. *The Franklin's Tale* could be read as a story about the patriarchal repression of female desire: Dorigen's desire is dangerously excessive, it breaks out threateningly against male control (including, in the black rocks speech, the control of a male God and his male defenders), but it is ultimately contained once more as the men collude together, united by the rivalry that divides them, leaving Dorigen silenced and *her* story untold.

That such views are unlikely to have been part of Chaucer's interpretation of the poem does not invalidate them. They become available to us as elements in a diagnosis of the culture that shaped and limited Chaucer's perceptions (just as our culture shapes and limits ours); and they may reasonably be felt to have a presence in the Tale, though not at the level of consciousness, simply because Chaucer, like any great poet, responded to the realities of life in ways that the ideologies of his age could not account for as well as in ways that they could. But we want to know too, as best we can, how Chaucer may have hoped his audience would understand Dorigen; and I suspect it would not have been in a way appealing to twentieth-century feminism. Dorigen's capacity for love, for desire, for passion and compassion, is genuine, and Chaucer surely wanted his readers to enter sympathetically into it; but it is just this that makes her incapable of exercising sensibly the *libertee* she is granted. She is not one of those classical heroines set up as models in her *compleynt*, and she would be less likeable if she were; fortunately she comes to see, after 'a day or tweye' (785) of lamentation, that the best thing is to follow her husband's orders, rigid and unimaginative though they may seem. Chaucer was capable of imagining heroic women, even women capable of heroic suffering, but Dorigen is not one of them. In *The Franklin's Tale* I cannot see that he questions what we now call patriarchy, though he allows that a woman may swear by her *trouthe*, whether married or unmarried, and, unlike Boccaccio, he does not exclude the possibility that a woman too could display *franchise*.

The Clerk of Orleans: Magic and Poetry

The Clerk of Orleans is conceived very differently from his counterpart in the *Filocolo*. Tebano is middle-aged and poverty-stricken; the Clerk is young and prosperous. To perform his magic, Tebano goes out alone at night, 'leaving behind his garments, bare-footed, with his disheveled hair hanging on his bare shoulders'; he performs sinister rituals with weird and disgusting objects, utters wild prayers, and is carried over Europe and Asia in 'a chariot drawn by two dragons'. He claims to possess great learning, but its origin is unmentioned, except for one reference to 'his books and other things necessary to his art'. The Clerk, by contrast, is a successful professional man, living comfortably in a house well provided with food, beds and servants, and he is repeatedly associated with learning drawn from books. In the early Middle Ages, when literacy had been largely confined to the Church, a clerk (Latin *clericus*) had meant a priest; by Chaucer's time, when literacy was more wide-spread, the term also referred to a student or learned man, and especially to one who knew Latin, the international language of the Church and of learning. Aurelius's brother thrice refers to a book as the link in his memory between Orleans and natural magic (452, 456, 463), and the Clerk establishes his clerkly status from the beginning by greeting his visitors in Latin (502). His initial display of skill takes place 'in his studie, ther as his bookes be' (535; cf. 542); and the process by which he makes the rocks disappear is associated not with pagan ritual but with the scientific terminology of medieval astrology.

In the Middle Ages magic and science were not separated; there was thus a real distinction between treating magic fantastically, as in the Breton lays or *Sir Gawain and the Green Knight*, and treating it realistically. The *Gawain*-poet shows no interest in the magical process by which Sir Bertilak acquired his second identity as a green knight; in *The Franklin's Tale*, however, though the ultimate details are left vague, attention is focused on magic itself, and it is treated as a scientific process. In Chaucer's time *magik natureel* (453) was distinguished from black magic; it was considered legitimate by many theological authorities, and was envisaged as a science employing not spirits but specialized knowledge of natural phenomena. The natural phenomena concerned in *The Franklin's Tale* are planetary influences, and there was nothing diabolic or illusory about those. It was believed that the seven 'planets' then known (including the sun and moon) influenced human life and earthly events according to their relationships and positions in the heavens. In the Tale's case, magic and science were indeed very close, for the moon and sun really do influence the tides, and could thus be responsible for concealing the rocks. This is what Aurelius prays Apollo to bring about, but prayer is not enough, and natural magic has to be resorted to.

This treatment of magic as science, however, is not unequivocal. Alongside it, throughout *The Franklin's Tale*, runs an alternative view of magic as illusion. The two views already coexist in the description of the book recalled by Aurelius's brother:

> Which book spak muchel of the operaciouns
> Touchinge the eighte and twenty mansiouns
> That longen to the moone, and swich folye
> As in oure dayes is nat worth a flye . . .　　(457–60)

A similar double attitude is expressed by the brother when he first thinks of this means of curing Aurelius's love-sickness:

> For I am siker that ther be sciences
> By whiche men make diverse apparences,
> Swiche as thise subtile tregetoures pleye.
> For ofte at feestes have I wel herd seye
> That tregetours, withinne an halle large,
> Have maad come in a water and a barge,
> And in the halle rowen up and doun.
> Somtime hath semed come a grim leoun;
> And somtime floures springe as in a mede;
> Somtime a vine, and grapes white and rede;
> Somtime a castel, al of lym and stoon;
> And whan hem liked, voided it anon.
> Thus semed it to every mannes sighte.　　(467–79)

These 'tregetour(e)s' are conjurers, creators of illusions, and the effects they produce are similar to elaborate entertainments devised for royal feasts in Chaucer's lifetime. The effects are 'apparences', designed to deceive the spectators' eyes—'Thus *semed* it to every mannes sighte'—but the *sciences* by which they are produced, like cinematic 'special effects' in our time, are a genuine technology of deceit, based on specialized skill and learning.

The same double emphasis occurs throughout. The ambiguous nature of magic is especially apparent in the feats that the Clerk performs for Aurelius on his arrival at his house:

> He shewed him, er he wente to sopeer,
> Forestes, parkes ful of wilde deer;
> Ther saugh he hertes with hir hornes hye,
> The gretteste that evere were seyn with ye.

> He saugh of hem an hondred slain with houndes,
> And somme with arwes blede of bittre woundes.
> He saugh, whan voided were thise wilde deer,
> Thise fauconers upon a fair river,
> That with hir haukes han the heron slain.
> Tho saugh he knightes justing in a plain;
> And after this he dide him swich plesaunce
> That he him shewed his lady on a daunce,
> On which himself he daunced, as him thoughte. (517–29)

The practical function of this demonstration is as bait, to entice Aurelius to hire the Clerk's services. The scenes shown, therefore, are chosen for their appeal to a young squire—hunting, hawking, jousting and dancing—but they are also visions of death and destruction. The dead and bleeding harts, the dead heron and the jousting knights can be read as a commentary on the nature of Aurelius's passion: it too is destructive, an urge towards death (as his prolonged sickness also indicates), not towards life. The vision of the harts is particularly effective, for they are bleeding from arrows, and the traditional metaphor of love as a death-dealing arrow has been applied only recently to Aurelius himself: 'But in his herte ay was the arwe kene' (440). The sudden disappearance of the last vision of Aurelius dancing with Dorigen further suggests the illusoriness of his passion, besides luring him further into the Clerk's power. Is this a different and more genuine kind of magic than that produced at feasts by 'tregetours'? We have no way of being certain, and the uncertainty perhaps belongs to the very nature of magic as Chaucer imagines it.

The final appearance of magic in the Tale is in the account of the experiment by which the Clerk makes the rocks vanish. He waits for a suitable opportunity, the planetary positions being vitally important, and correctly chooses January, when the moon is in a particularly powerful position. As with the book the brother remembered, scorn is cast on the science used: it is *illusioun* or *apparence* (592, 593), and the Clerk's 'supersticious cursednesse' (600) belongs to the realm of the 'illusiouns and . . . meschaunces' practised by 'hethen folk' in those times (620–1). At the same time, fascination is shown with astrology, in an ostentatious show of its technical jargon. The ambiguity of magic remains to the very end, the last two lines of the account being that 'thurgh his magik, for a wyke or tweye, / It semed that alle the rokkes were aweye' (623–4). The statement that 'the rokkes were aweye' comes emphatically as the long description's climax, but is still preceded by 'It semed'. We might expect the ambiguity to be resolved when Aurelius has to show that the task set by Dorigen is complete, but this is not what happens. We are told of Aurelius's gratitude when 'he knew that ther was noon obstacle, / That voided were thise rokkes everichon' (628–9), but we are not told that he went to see for himself. Similarly, Aurelius actually invites Dorigen to check that the task has been performed—'And if ye vouche sauf, ye may go see' (662)—yet she never does so. And even if Aurelius and Dorigen did 'go see' that the rocks had been 'voided', could they trust their eyes, when the illusions produced at feasts can also be 'voided'—'Thus semed it to every mannes sighte' (478, 479)? There is no way of deciding whether the Clerk's magic was 'really' *natureel* or *illusioun*, for we know only what we are told in the Tale. Its ambiguity is essential and intentional, for it must at once produce the effect of removing the rocks and indicate that, even in having this miracle performed, Aurelius is still pursuing an illusion.

Of the Tale's characters, only the Clerk is not associated

with extreme emotions. From the moment he enters the story, he seems in perfect control of himself and detached from the emotions of others: he calmly announces his mysterious knowledge as to why Aurelius and his brother have come to Orleans, and when the brother asks him about their former student acquaintances, he equally calmly informs him of their deaths, and it is the brother, not he, who weeps 'ful ofte many a teere' (510). He is once said to feel 'routhe' for Aurelius (589), but his chief motive is apparently to earn the largest fee possible: having tempted Aurelius with the demonstration in his study, he bargains hard, and it emerges that his minimum demand of a 'thousand pound' (552) is actually a thousand pounds in weight of pure gold (888)—a huge sum, equivalent to several million modern pounds sterling. In the *gentillesse* competition, we are told nothing of any inner feelings that move him to be generous, but only of his wish to show that a clerk can be as *gentil* as a knight or squire. He departs as mysteriously as he entered, with a brisk 'good day' (947) that still reveals nothing of his inner life. All that is certain about his desires is that he likes food (514, 537–45, 946) and money, and is proud of his skill and his reputation.

It is hard, perhaps, to see how the Clerk can be a competitor for the title of 'mooste fre'; but he has no need to compete with the other characters, because he exists on a higher plane than theirs. It is his magic, ambiguous though it may be, that manipulates them and shapes the story, and there is a sense in which his role corresponds to the poet's own, not unlike that of Shakespeare's magician Prospero in *The Tempest*. Geoffrey of Vinsauf's *Poetria Nova*, a rhetorical textbook known to Chaucer, compares poetic art to conjuring: 'Art plays, as it were, the conjurer: causes the last to be first, the future to be present, the oblique to be straight, the remote to become near . . .';[1] it also makes many comparisons between poetry and the delicious food that means so much to the Clerk that he regards it as sufficient reward for his efforts (946). The demonstration mounted in his study forms a visual summary of the favourite topics of medieval courtly romances (hunting, hawking, knights jousting, a squire dancing with the lady he loves). As one scholar puts it, 'The image of a magician in his study is meant to evoke the image of a poet among his books, a comparison that is for poetry as troubling as it is exalting.'[2] Is poetry magic or illusion, a beneficent trans-formation of reality to remove its worst dangers or 'super-sticious cursednesse' (600)? Is poetic phraseology such as 'the brighte sonne loste his hewe; / For th'orisonte hath reft the sonne his light' really no more than a deceptive cloak for the grim truth that 'it was night' (344–6)? 'The image of *a* poet', not necessarily of Chaucer: a 'yong clerk rominge by himself' (501), not the busy middle-aged Chaucer who wrote *The Franklin's Tale*. Yet it is easy to see parallels between Chaucer and the Clerk of Orleans: Chaucer too was a learned and prosperous professional, a man whose status depended on skill rather than birth, a producer of fictions for his social superiors, an accomplished artist who feared that his art might be trivial and even damnable, a man who habitually wrote about romantic love and yet always presented himself as knowing it only from books, not from his own feelings—that is how Chaucer appears in

[1] *Poetria Nova of Geoffrey of Vinsauf*, trans. Margaret F. Nims (Pontifical Institute of Medieval Studies, Toronto, 1967).

[2] V. A. Kolve, 'Rocky Shores and Pleasure Gardens: Poetry vs. Magic in Chaucer's *Franklin's Tale*', in *Poetics: Theory and Practice in Medieval English Poetry*, ed. Piero Boitani and Anna Torti (D. S. Brewer, 1991).

Introduction

Troilus and Criseyde, as one who writes 'of no senti-
ment . . . But out of Latin' and who 'speaks of love
unfeelingly' (*Troilus*, Book II, Prologue). It is perhaps just
by chance that the Clerk speaks the only specifically
Christian phrase attributed to any of these pagan characters, when he swears 'so God him save' (551) that he will
not accept less than a thousand pounds, but it would be
pleasant to think that at that moment, consciously or
unconsciously, Chaucer was identifying with him.

THE TALE AND ITS TELLER

The relation of the various *Canterbury Tales* to the pilgrims who tell them has aroused much disagreement. In the
finest of the early manuscripts, the Ellesmere, pictures of
the pilgrims as described in the *General Prologue* are placed
not in the Prologue itself but alongside the tales they tell;
but it was not until the early twentieth century that G. L.
Kittredge (see page 19, footnote) proposed a systematic
relationship between tales and tellers by suggesting that
'*The Canterbury Tales* is a kind of Human Comedy' and
that the tales should be regarded as 'primarily significant . . . because they illustrate the speaker's character and
opinions'. This proposal gave a new direction to Chaucer
criticism; its implications were worked out over many
years, and it continues to be fruitful. But over the years,
too, objections have emerged; Kittredge seems to imply
that tellers are intrinsically more interesting than tales
(which is surely not so), and while many would agree that
in certain cases (such as the Pardoner, the Canon's
Yeoman, and the Wife of Bath), tales and tellers throw

valuable light on each other, in many other cases the connection is only generic (the Knight tells a knightly tale, the Miller 'a cherles tale in his manere'), and in still others (such as the Man of Law and the Physician) extremely fine-spun argument is needed to establish a link at all. A major problem is that, given a structure in which it is *possible* for a tale and its teller to be significantly linked, our own imaginations set to work, and they may well create links rather than discover them. In practice, the interpretative use made of connections between pilgrims and tales has frequently been to stabilize a tale by attributing any anomalous elements to the teller's 'biases' and 'misunderstandings'; but the anomalies may be a tale's most interesting features, and the effect of this method is too often reductive, using a supposedly ironic treatment of the teller to show that the tale 'really' means whatever the reader prefers.

In the case of the Franklin and his Tale, I once believed that close and subtle connections existed, but have now come to suspect that these were largely the product of my imagination. More important, I find *The Franklin's Tale*, with its dynamic interaction of themes and its shifting points of view, more interesting than hypotheses about the 'character and opinions' of the Franklin. The *General Prologue* portrait of the Franklin (printed on pages 79–80 below) is fascinating in itself, but not everything in it bears significantly on the Tale that comes several thousand lines later. The portrait strongly emphasizes the Franklin's hospitality and his love of food and drink, and we may see reflections of these in the vignette of Janus enjoying wine and 'brawen of the tusked swyn' (582) at Christmas and in the Orleans

Clerk's similar interests: compare his sharp address to his
squire—

> Is redy oure soper?
> Almoost an houre it is, I undertake,
> Sith I yow bad oure soper for to make . . .   (538–40)

—with the indication of a similarly demanding attitude on
the Franklin's part:

> Wo was his cook but if his sauce were
> Poynaunt and sharp, and redy al his geere. (*GP* 353–4)

But we are also told that the Franklin was

> Epicurus owene sone,
> That heeld opinioun that pleyn delit
> Was verray felicitee parfit.   (*GP* 338–40)

(A devoted follower of Epicurus, who took the view that
sheer pleasure was true perfect happiness.) Given that
felicitee tends to mean 'heavenly bliss', this conveys severe
moral reproof, and it is hard to find such harsh criticism
echoed in the Tale. More significant, perhaps, is what is not
explicit in the portrait, namely the Franklin's social status.
Exactly what 'franklin' implied in Chaucer's time is a
matter of scholarly controversy. The *General Prologue*
portrait indicates that this franklin had occupied major
offices usually held by knights—member of parliament,
presiding justice of the peace, sheriff, county court
pleader—and some have argued that franklins were equivalent in status to knights and squires; others find evidence
that 'franklins rarely rose beyond the lower ranks of the
office-holding hierarchy' and that 'contemporaries would
have had little difficulty in distinguishing the franklins
from their superiors, the knights'.[1] The very difficulty of

---

[1] Nigel Saul, 'The Social Status of Chaucer's Franklin: A Recon-
sideration', *Medium Ævum*, 52 (1983).

placing this unusually successful franklin in a late-medieval social structure that was less fixed than the traditional terms available to describe it may be a significant feature of the portrait.

Certainly, when we reach *The Franklin's Prologue* (in which I include the link-passage headed 'Heere folwen the wordes of the Frankeleyn to the Squier . . .'), social status emerges as an important issue. The Squire, introduced in the *General Prologue* as the Knight's son, has been telling a tale perfectly in keeping with his portrait as a typical young courtier—a chivalric romance, exotic in setting and full of improbable wonders, concerning characters who are models of aristocratic behaviour. This marvellous story is told with naïve enthusiasm: all the characters are perfect of their kind, and wonders are heaped breathlessly on wonders—a brass horse that carries its rider wherever he chooses, a mirror that reveals friends and enemies and true and false lovers, a ring that grants understanding of bird language, a sword that pierces any armour but also heals the wound, a hawk that has an unhappy love-affair. The Squire, entangled in the complications of his narrative, ends Part II of his Tale with a desperate attempt to pull the threads together and an enthusiastic 'trailer' for forthcoming 'merveilles':

> Thus lete I Canacee hir hauk keping;
> I wol namoore as now speke of hir ring,
> Til it com eft to purpos for to seyn
> How that this faucon gat hir love ageyn
> Repentant, as the storie telleth us,
> By mediacion of Cambalus,
> The kinges sone, of which that I yow tolde,
> But hennesforth I wol my proces holde
> To speken of aventures and of batailles,
> That nevere yet was herd so grete merveilles!
> First wol I telle yow . . .

> And after wol I speke . . .
> And after wol I speke . . .
> And ther I lefte I wol ageyn biginne.

He begins on Part III—

> Appollo whirleth up his chaar so hye
> Til that the god Mercurius hous, the slye—

—but at this point, with Apollo (the god of poetic inspiration as well as the sun) in mid-air, the text halts abruptly, and the next words are spoken by the Franklin. It is as if Apollo has been shot down by a ground-to-air missile, and it seems likely that Chaucer meant to have the Franklin interrupting the Squire, just as elsewhere the Knight interrupts the Monk and the Host interrupts Chaucer himself.

If so, the interruption is tactful. *The Squire's Tale* has surely lasted long enough, but the Franklin says nothing of this, only praising the Squire for his intelligence and his 'feeling' eloquence (4), fervently wishing him well, and saying how much he has enjoyed listening to him. Yet the Franklin's praise sounds somewhat patronizing. He stresses the finality of his own judgment— '*I* preise wel thy wit, . . . *I* have greet deyntee' (2, 9)—while his 'consideringe thy yowthe' (3), with the deliberating pause before it in the phrase 'Quod the Frankeleyn', undermines his eulogy. The patronizing attitude is continued in 'If that thou live' (7), deferring the Squire's achievement to an uncertain future. We seem to hear, in the Franklin's opening lines, the tact of a man determined to assert his own social standing.

The Franklin praises the Squire as having performed 'gentilly' (2), thus introducing the theme of *gentillesse*, which will be of central importance in *The Franklin's Tale*. Here the precariousness of the Franklin's own social status becomes significant. Is a franklin in a position to assess a squire's *gentillesse*? In the words that follow, the uncertainty is developed not simply as an objective fact about franklins but as an element in this Franklin's view of himself:

> I have a sone, and by the Trinitee,
> I hadde levere than twenty pound worth lond,
> Though it right now were fallen in myn hond,
> He were a man of swich discrecioun
> As that ye been. Fy on possessioun,
> But if a man be vertuous withal!
> I have my sone snybbed, and yet shal,
> For he to vertu listeth nat entende;
> But for to pleye at dees, and to despende
> And lese al that he hath, is his usage.
> And he hath levere talken with a page
> Than to comune with any gentil wight
> Where he myghte lerne gentillesse aright.   (10–22)

Seeing the Knight's son makes the Franklin remember his own, and the comparison is much to his son's disadvantage; yet to make it is to put the two young men on the same footing. The Franklin envies on his son's behalf the Squire's *discrecioun, vertu* and *gentillesse*, but in doing so he implicitly claims that his son ought to possess these aristocratic virtues. He would rather his son matched the Squire than acquire land worth twenty pounds a year, even if it came into his possession at this very moment—an expression that betrays his own assumption that moral values are commensurate with material values, and is followed by a denial of the importance of *possessioun* without *vertu* that reveals the very assumption it repudiates. He imagines that scolding his son might make him pursue *vertu* rather than lose his money at dice, and learn a correct view of *gentillesse* by conversing with a 'gentil wight' (21); the subtext is that if only his son *won* at dice he might find it less annoying, and that what is at stake in the comparison between a mere page and a 'gentil wight' may be social prestige rather than *vertu*. With delicate irony, these lines allow the Franklin to expose muddled values with no awareness of what he is doing.

The Host, a plain blunt man, recognizes the Franklin's pretensions clearly enough, and feels that he has invoked *gentillesse* far too often. He reminds him of the agreement underlying the tale-telling competition; and the Franklin responds with strangely modest deference. When he addresses the Host in the polite second-person plural, saying,

> I prey to God that it may ʾ sen yow;
> Thanne woot I wel that it is goʊu yʾ w,   (35–6)

is he speaking with genuine flattery or with an irony that turns the tables on the irony with which the poet has just been treating him? The reader is left free to judge, and the Franklin moves into his Prologue proper. Referring in his very next line to 'Thise olde *gentil* Britouns', he defies the Host's prohibition, and then, as if to match the Host's bluntness, makes a parade of his own ignorance of rhetoric. Yet the very words in which he denies rhetorical skill display it ostentatiously. Beginning a literary work by apologizing for one's own incapacity is a rhetorical device called *diminutio*, recommended by textbooks as a way of capturing the audience's goodwill. 'Thing that I speke, it moot be bare and pleyn' (48): bareness and plainness are skilfully evoked in an entirely monosyllabic line, but in the following lines he goes on to repeat himself in showily figurative terms. This trick of repeating the same ideas in

NOTE ON THE TEXT

The text which follows is based upon that of F. N. Robinson (*The Complete Works of Geoffrey Chaucer*, 2nd ed., 1957). The punctuation has been revised, with special reference to the exclamation marks. Spelling has been partly rationalized, by substituting *i* for *y* wherever the change aids the modern reader and does not affect the semantic value of the word. Thus *smylyng* becomes 'smiling', and *nyghtyngale* 'nightingale', but *wyn* (wine), *lyk* (like), and *fyr* (fire) are allowed to stand.

No accentuation has been provided in this text, for two reasons. First, because it produces a page displeasing to the eye; secondly, because it no longer seems necessary or entirely reliable in the light of modern scholarship. It is not now thought that the later works of Chaucer were written in a ten-syllable line from which no variation was permissible. The correct reading of a line of Chaucer is now seen to be more closely related to the correct reading of a comparable line of prose with phrasing suited to the rhythms of speech. This allows the reader to be more flexible in his interpretation of the line, and makes it unreasonably pedantic to provide a rigid system of accentuation.

NOTE ON PRONUNCIATION

These equivalences are intended to offer only a rough guide. For further detail, see *An Introduction to Chaucer*.

SHORT VOWELS

ă represents the sound now written *u*, as in 'cut'
ĕ as in modern 'set'
ĭ as in modern 'is'
ŏ as in modern 'top'
ŭ as in modern 'put' (not as in 'cut')
final -*e* represents the neutral vowel sound in '*a*bout' or 'attent*io*n'. It is silent when the next word in the line begins with a vowel or an *h*

Note on the Text

ā as in modern 'car' (not as in 'name')

ē (open—i.e. where the equivalent modern word is spelt with *ea*) as in modern 'there'

ē (close—i.e. where the equivalent modern word is spelt with *ee* or *e*) represents the sound now written *a* as in 'take'

ī as in modern 'machine' (not as in 'like')

ō (open—i.e. where the equivalent modern vowel is pronounced as in 'br*o*ther', 'm*oo*d', or 'g*oo*d') represents the sound now written *aw* as in 'fawn'

ō (close—i.e. where the equivalent modern vowel is pronounced as in 'road') as in modern 'note'

ū as in French *tu* or German *Tür*

DIPHTHONGS

ai and *ei* both roughly represent the sound now written *i* or *y* as in 'die' or 'dye'

au and *aw* both represent the sound now written *ow* or *ou* as in 'now' or 'pounce'

ou and *ow* have two pronunciations: as in *through* where the equivalent modern vowel is pronounced as in 'through' or 'mouse'; and as in *pounce* where the equivalent modern vowel is pronounced as in 'know' or 'thought'

WRITING OF VOWELS AND DIPHTHONGS

A long vowel is often indicated by doubling, as in *roote* or *eek*. The *ŭ* sound is sometimes represented by an *o* as in *yong*. The *au* sound is sometimes represented by an *a*, especially before *m* or *n*, as in *cha(u)mbre* or *cha(u)nce*.

CONSONANTS

Largely as in modern English, except that many consonants now silent were still pronounced. *Gh* was pronounced as in Scottish 'lo*ch*', and both consonants should be pronounced in such groups as the following: '*gn*acchen', '*kn*ave', 'wo*rd*', 'fo*lk*', '*wr*ong'.

THE PORTRAIT OF THE FRANKLIN

From *The General Prologue*, lines 333–62

[handwritten annotations: rhyming couplets / iambic pentameters (Shakespeare); Man of substance. prosperous. public figure. important. Not out of top drawer. 3rd rank down from knight. of serjeant of law – came before him]

A FRANKELEYN was in his compaignye.
Whit was his berd as is the dayesye;
Of his complexioun he was sangwin.
Wel loved he by the morwe a sop in wyn;
To liven in delit was evere his wone,
For he was Epicurus owene sone,
That heeld opinioun that pleyn delit
Was verray felicitee parfit.
An housholdere, and that a greet, was he;
Seint Julian he was in his contrée.
His breed, his ale, was alweys after oon;
A bettre envined man was nowher noon.
Withoute bake mete was nevere his hous
Of fissh and flessh, and that so plentevous,
It snewed in his hous of mete and drinke,
Of alle deyntees that men koude thinke.
After the sondry sesons of the yeer,
So chaunged he his mete and his soper.
Ful many a fat partrich hadde he in muwe,
And many a breem and many a luce in stuwe.
Wo was his cook but if his sauce were
Poynaunt and sharp, and redy al his geere.
His table dormant in his halle alway
Stood redy covered al the longe day.
At sessiouns ther was he lord and sire;

[handwritten annotations: company; beard; daisy; temperament; sanguine (red blood) and dipped in wine; morning a piece of; pleasure; ardent follower of Epicurus; total pleasure; truly perfect happiness; own wine and property; distinguished, great; country; Patron St of hospitality; up to the same standard; stocked with wine; food; snowed (piled); blizzard of meat & drink; delicacies; in accordance with the seasons he changed his meat & ale; coop; bream (fat fish); pike; fish-pond; this cook was not popular unless; pungent spicy; everything always had to be ready; broad table; great hall – main entertaining, feasting area; laid; He presided over the justices of the peace]

Ful ofte time he was knight of the shire.
An anlaas and a gipser al of silk
Heeng at his girdel, whit as morne milk.
A shirreve hadde he been, and a contour.
Was nowher swich a worthy vavasour.

complexioun temperament   *morwe* morning
To liven . . . felicitee parfit see pages 69–70
Seint Julian patron saint of hospitality
after oon up to the same standard
envined stocked with wine   *mete* food
snewed snowed, proliferated   *muwe* coop
luce pike   *stuwe* fish-pond   *poynaunt* pungent
table dormant fixed table
At sessions . . . sire he presided over the justices of the peace
knight of the shire member of parliament for his county
anlaas dagger   *gipser* purse   *shirreve* sheriff
contour pleader in county court   *vavasour* landholder.

80

THE FRANKLIN'S PROLOGUE

Heere folwen the wordes of the Frankeleyn to the
Squier, and the wordes of the Hoost to the Frankeleyn.

'In feith, Squier, thow hast thee wel yquit
And gentilly. I preise wel thy wit,'
Quod the Frankeleyn, 'consideringe thy yowthe,
So feelingly thou spekest, sire, I allow the.
As to my doom, ther is noon that is heere
Of eloquence that shal be thy peere,
If that thou live; God yeve thee good chaunce,
And in vertu sende thee continuaunce!
For of thy speche I have greet deyntee.
I have a sone, and by the Trinitee,   10
I hadde levere than twenty pound worth lond,
Though it right now were fallen in myn hond,
He were a man of swich discrecioun
As that yé been. Fy on possessioun,
But if a man be vertuous withal!
I have my sone snybbed, and yet shal,
For he to vertu listeth nat entende;
But for to pleye at dees, and to despende
And lese al that he hath, is his usage.
And he hath levere talken with a page   20
Than to comune with any gentil wight
Where he mighte lerne gentilesse aright.'
'Straw for youre gentillesse!' quod oure Hoost.
'What, Frankeleyn! pardee, sire, wel thou woost
That ech of yow moot tellen atte leste
A tale or two, or breken his biheste.'
'That knowe I wel, sire,' quod the Frankeleyn.

81

'I prey yow, haveth me nat in desdeyn,
Though to this man I speke a word or two.'
30   'Telle on thy tale withouten wordes mo.'
'Gladly, sire Hoost,' quod he, 'I wole obeye
Unto your wil; now herkneth what I seye.
I wol yow nat contrarien in no wise
As fer as that my wittes wol suffise.
I prey to God that it may plesen yow;
Thanne woot I wel that it is good ynow.'

The Prologe of the Frankeleyns Tale

Thise olde gentil Britouns in hir dayes
Of diverse aventures maden layes,
Rimeyed in hir firste Briton tonge;
40   Whiche layes with hir instrumentz they songe,
Or elles redden hem for hir plesaunce,
And oon of hem have I in remembraunce,
Which I shal seyn with good wil as I kan.
But sires, by cause I am a burel man,
At my biginning first I yow biseche,
Have me excused of my rude speche.
I lerned nevere rethorik, certeyn;
Thing that I speke, it moot be bare and pleyn.
I sleep nevere on the Mount of Pernaso,
50   Ne lerned Marcus Tullius Scithero.
Colours ne knowe I none, withouten drede,
But swiche colours as growen in the mede,
Or elles swiche as men dye or peynte.
Colours of rethorik been to me queynte;
My spirit feeleth noght of swich mateere.
But if yow list, my tale shul ye heere.

THE FRANKLIN'S TALE

In Armorik, that called is Britaine,
Ther was a knight that loved and dide his paine
To serve a lady in his beste wise;
And many a labour, many a greet emprise   60
He for his lady wroghte, er she were wonne.
For she was oon the faireste under sonne,
And eek therto comen of so heigh kinrede
That wel unnethes dorste this knight, for drede,
Telle hire his wo, his peyne, and his distresse.
But atte laste she, for his worthinesse,
And namely for his meke obeisaunce,
Hath swich a pitee caught of his penaunce
That prively she fil of his accord
To take him for hir housbonde and hir lord,   70
Of swich lordshipe as men han over hir wives.
And for to lede the moore in blisse hir lives,
Of his free wil he swoor hire as a knight
That nevere in al his lyf he, day ne night,
Ne sholde upon him take no maistrie
Again hir wil, ne kithe hire jalousie,
But hire obeye, and folwe hir wil in al,
As any lovere to his lady shal,
Save that the name of soverainetee,
That wolde he have for shame of his degree.   80
  She thanked him, and with ful greet humblesse
She seyde, 'Sire, sith of youre gentillesse
Ye profre me to have so large a reine,
Ne wolde nevere God bitwixe us tweyne,
As in my gilt, were outher werre or stryf.

83

Sire, I wol be youre humble trewe wyf,
Have heer my trouthe, til that myn herte breste.'
Thus been they bothe in quiete and in reste.

    For o thing, sires, saufly dar I seye,
90 That freendes everich oother moot obeye,
If they wol longe holden compaignye.
Love wol nat been constreyned by maistrye.
Whan maistrie comth, the God of Love anon
Beteth his winges, and farewel, he is gon!
Love is a thing as any spirit free.
Wommen, of kinde, desiren libertee,
And nat to been constreyned as a thral;
And so doon men, if I sooth seyen shal.
Looke who that is moost pacient in love,
100 He is at his avantage al above.
Pacience is an heigh vertu, certeyn,
For it venquisseth, as thise clerkes seyn,
Thinges that rigour sholde nevere atteyne.
For every word men may nat chide or pleyne.
Lerneth to suffre, or elles, so moot I goon,
Ye shul it lerne, wher so ye wole or noon;
For in this world, certein, ther no wight is
That he ne dooth or seith somtime amis.
Ire, siknesse, or constellacioun,
110 Wyn, wo, or chaunginge of complexioun
Causeth ful ofte to doon amis or speken.
On every wrong a man may nat be wreken.
After the time moste be temperaunce
To every wight that kan on governaunce.
And therfore hath this wise, worthy knight,
To live in ese, suffrance hire bihight,
And she to him ful wisly gan to swere

84

That nevere sholde ther be defaute in here.
  Heere may men seen an humble, wys accord;
Thus hath she take hir servant and hir lord—   120
Servant in love, and lord in mariage.
Thanne was he bothe in lordshipe and servage.
Servage? nay, but in lordshipe above,
Sith he hath bothe his lady and his love;
His lady, certes, and his wyf also,
The which that lawe of love acordeth to.
And whan he was in this prosperitee,
Hoom with his wyf he gooth to his contree,
Nat fer fro Pedmark, ther his dwelling was,
Where as he liveth in blisse and in solas.   130
  Who koude telle, but he hadde wedded be,
The joye, the ese, and the prosperitee
That is bitwixe an housbonde and his wyf?
A yeer and moore lasted this blisful lyf,
Til that the knight of which I speke of thus,
That of Kayrrud was cleped Arveragus,
Shoop him to goon and dwelle a yeer or tweyne
In Engelond, that cleped was eek Briteyne,
To seke in armes worshipe and honour;
For al his lust he sette in swich labour;   140
And dwelled there two yeer, the book seith thus.
  Now wol I stynten of this Arveragus,
And speken I wole of Dorigen his wyf,
That loveth hire housbonde as hire hertes lyf.
For his absence wepeth she and siketh,
As doon thise noble wives whan hem liketh.
She moorneth, waketh, waileth, fasteth, pleyneth;
Desir of his presence hire so destreyneth
That al this wide world she sette at noght.

150 Hire freendes, whiche that knewe hir hevy thoght,
Conforten hire in al that ever they may.
They prechen hire, they telle hire night and day
That causelees she sleeth hirself, allas!
And every confort possible in this cas
They doon to hire with al hire bisinesse,
Al for to make hire leve hire hevinesse.

By proces, as ye knowen everichoon,
Men may so longe graven in a stoon
Til som figure therinne emprented be.
160 So longe han they conforted hire, til she
Received hath, by hope and by resoun,
The emprenting of hire consolacioun,
Thurgh which hir grete sorwe gan aswage;
She may nat alwey duren in swich rage.

And eek Arveragus, in al this care,
Hath sent hire lettres hoom of his welfare,
And that he wol come hastily again;
Or elles hadde this sorwe hir herte slain.

Hire freendes sawe hir sorwe gan to slake,
170 And preyde hire on knees, for Goddes sake,
To come and romen hire in compaignye,
Awey to drive hire derke fantasye.
And finally she graunted that requeste,
For wel she saugh that it was for the beste.

Now stood hire castel faste by the see,
And often with hire freendes walketh shee,
Hire to disporte, upon the bank an heigh,
Where as she many a ship and barge seigh
Seillinge hir cours, where as hem liste go.
180 But thanne was that a parcel of hire wo,
For to hirself ful ofte, 'Allas!' seith she,

86

'Is ther no ship, of so manye as I se,
Wol bringen hom my lord? Thanne were myn herte
Al warisshed of his bittre peynes smerte.'

    Another time ther wolde she sitte and thinke,
And caste hir eyen dounward fro the brinke.
But whan she saugh the grisly rokkes blake,
For verray feere so wolde hir herte quake
That on hire feet she mighte hire noght sustene.
Thanne wolde she sitte adoun upon the grene,   190
And pitously into the see biholde,
And seyn right thus, with sorweful sikes colde:
    'Eterne God, that thurgh thy purveiaunce
Ledest the world by certein governaunce,
In idel, as men seyn, ye no thing make.
But, Lord, thise grisly feendly rokkes blake,
That semen rather a foul confusion
Of werk than any fair creacion
Of swich a parfit wys God and a stable,
Why han ye wroght this werk unresonable?   200
For by this werk, south, north, ne west, ne eest,
Ther nis yfostred man, ne brid, ne beest;
It dooth no good, to my wit, but anoyeth.
Se ye nat, Lord, how mankinde it destroyeth?
An hundred thousand bodies of mankinde
Han rokkes slain, al be they nat in minde,
Which mankinde is so fair part of thy werk
That thou it madest lyk to thyn owene merk.
Thanne semed it ye hadde a greet chiertee
Toward mankinde; but how thanne may it bee   210
That ye swiche meenes make it to destroyen,
Whiche meenes do no good, but evere anoyen?
I woot wel clerkes wol seyn as hem leste,

87

By argumentz, that al is for the beste,
Though I ne kan the causes nat yknowe.
But thilke God that made wind to blowe
As kepe my lord! this my conclusion:
To clerkes lete I al disputison.
But wolde God that alle thise rokkes blake
220   Were sonken into helle for his sake!
Thise rokkes sleen myn herte for the feere.'
Thus wolde she seyn, with many a pitous teere.

Hire freendes sawe that it was no disport
To romen by the see, but disconfort,
And shopen for to pleyen somwher elles.
They leden hire by riveres and by welles,
And eek in othere places delitables;
They dauncen, and they pleyen at ches and tables.

So on a day, right in the morwe-tide,
230   Unto a gardyn that was ther biside,
In which that they hadde maad hir ordinaunce
Of vitaille and of oother purveiaunce,
They goon and pleye hem al the longe day.
And this was on the sixte morwe of May,
Which May hadde peynted with his softe shoures
This gardyn ful of leves and of floures;
And craft of mannes hand so curiously
Arrayed hadde this gardyn, trewely,
That nevere was ther gardyn of swich prys,
240   But if it were the verray paradis.
The odour of floures and the fresshe sighte
Wolde han maked any herte lighte
That evere was born, but if to greet siknesse,
Or to greet sorwe, helde it in distresse;
So ful it was of beautee with plesaunce.

At after-diner gonne they to daunce,
And singe also, save Dorigen allone,
Which made alwey hir compleint and hir moone,
For she ne saugh him on the daunce go
That was hir housbonde and hir love also.   250
But nathelees she moste a time abide,
And with good hope lete hir sorwe slide.

  Upon this daunce, amonges othere men,
Daunced a squier biforn Dorigen,
That fressher was and jolier of array,
As to my doom, than is the month of May.
He singeth, daunceth, passinge any man
That is, or was, sith that the world bigan.
Therwith he was, if men sholde him discrive,
Oon of the beste faringe man on live;   260
Yong, strong, right vertuous, and riche, and wys,
And wel biloved, and holden in greet prys.
And shortly, if the sothe I tellen shal,
Unwiting of this Dorigen at al,
This lusty squier, servant to Venus,
Which that ycleped was Aurelius,
Hadde loved hire best of any creature
Two yeer and moore, as was his aventure,
But nevere dorste he tellen hire his grevaunce.
Withouten coppe he drank al his penaunce.   270
He was despeyred; no thing dorste he seye,
Save in his songes somwhat wolde he wreye
His wo, as in a general compleyning;
He seyde he lovede, and was biloved no thing.
Of swich matere made he manye layes,
Songes, compleintes, roundels, virelayes,
How that he dorste nat his sorwe telle,

But langwissheth as a furye dooth in helle;
And die he moste, he seyde, as dide Ekko
For Narcisus, that dorste nat telle hir wo.
In oother manere than ye heere me seye,
Ne dorste he nat to hire his wo biwreye,
Save that, paraventure, somtime at daunces,
Ther yonge folk kepen hir observaunces,
It may wel be he looked on hir face
In swich a wise as man that asketh grace;
But nothing wiste she of his entente.

    Nathelees it happed, er they thennes wente,
By cause that he was hire neighebour,
And was a man of worshipe and honour,
And hadde yknowen him of time yoore,
They fille in speche; and forth, moore and moore,
Unto his purpos drough Aurelius,
And whan he saugh his time, he seyde thus:

    'Madame,' quod he, 'by God that this world made,
So that I wiste it mighte youre herte glade,
I wolde that day that youre Arveragus
Wente over the see, that I, Aurelius,
Hadde went ther nevere I sholde have come again.
For wel I woot my service is in vain;
My gerdon is but bresting of myn herte.
Madame, reweth upon my peynes smerte;
For with a word ye may me sleen or save.
Heere at youre feet God wolde that I were grave!
I ne have as now no leiser moore to seye;
Have mercy, sweete, or ye wol do me deye.'

    She gan to looke upon Aurelius:
'Is this youre wil,' quod she, 'and sey ye thus?
Nevere erst,' quod she, 'ne wiste I what ye mente.

290

300

280

But now, Aurelie, I knowe youre entente,
By thilke God that yaf me soule and lyf,
Ne shal I nevere been untrewe wyf
In word ne werk, as fer as I have wit;
I wol been his to whom that I am knit.
Taak this for final answere as of me.'
But after that in pley thus seyde she:

'Aurelie,' quod she, 'by heighe God above,
Yet wolde I graunte yow to been youre love,
Sin I yow se so pitously complaine.
Looke what day that endelong Britaine   320
Ye remoeve alle the rokkes, stoon by stoon,
That they ne lette ship ne boot to goon,—
I seye, whan ye han maad the coost so clene
Of rokkes that ther nis no stoon ysene,
Thanne wol I love yow best of any man,
Have heer my trouthe, in al that evere I kan.'
'Is ther noon oother grace in yow?' quod he.
'No, by that Lord,' quod she, 'that maked me.
For wel I woot that it shal never bitide.
Lat swiche folies out of youre herte slide.   330
What deyntee sholde a man han in his lyf
For to go love another mannes wyf,
That hath hir body whan so that him liketh?'
Aurelius ful ofte soore siketh;
Wo was Aurelie whan that he this herde,
And with a sorweful herte he thus answerde:
'Madame,' quod he, 'this were an inpossible!
Thanne moot I die of sodeyn deth horrible.'
And with that word he turned him anon.
Tho coome hir othere freendes many oon,   340
And in the aleyes romeden up and doun,

And nothing wiste of this conclusioun,
But sodeynly bigonne revel newe
Til that the brighte sonne loste his hewe;
For th'orisonte hath reft the sonne his light—
This is as muche to seye as it was night.
And hoom they goon in joye and in solas,
Save oonly wrecche Aurelius, allas!
He to his hous is goon with sorweful herte.
350   He seeth he may nat fro his deeth asterte;
Him semed that he felte his herte colde.
Up to the hevene his handes he gan holde,
And on his knowes bare he sette him doun,
And in his raving seyde his orisoun.
For verray wo out of his wit he breyde.
He niste what he spak, but thus he seyde;
With pitous herte his pleynt hath he bigonne
Unto the goddes, and first unto the sonne:

He seyde, 'Appollo, god and governour
360   Of every plaunte, herbe, tree, and flour,
That yevest, after thy declinacion,
To ech of hem his time and his seson,
As thyn herberwe chaungeth lowe or heighe,
Lord Phebus, cast thy merciable eighe
On wrecche Aurelie, which that am but lorn.
Lo, lord! my lady hath my deeth ysworn
Withoute gilt, but thy benignitee
Upon my dedly herte have som pitee.
For wel I woot, lord Phebus, if yow lest,
370   Ye may me helpen, save my lady, best.
Now voucheth sauf that I may yow devise
How that I may been holpen and in what wise.
Youre blisful suster, Lucina the sheene,

That of the see is chief goddesse and queene
(Though Neptunus have deitee in the see,
Yet emperisse aboven him is she),
Ye knowen wel, lord, that right as hir desir
Is to be quiked and lighted of youre fir,
For which she folweth yow ful bisily,
Right so the see desireth naturelly   380
To folwen hire, as she that is goddesse
Bothe in the see and riveres moore and lesse.
Wherfore, lord Phebus, this is my requeste—
Do this miracle, or do myn herte breste—
That now next at this opposicion
Which in the signe shal be of the Leon,
As preieth hire so greet a flood to bringe
That five fadme at the leeste it oversprynge
The hyeste rokke in Armorik Briteyne;
And lat this flood endure yeres tweyne.   390
Thanne certes to my lady may I seye,
"Holdeth youre heste, the rokkes been aweye."
    Lord Phebus, dooth this miracle for me.
Preye hire she go no faster cours than ye;
I seye, preyeth your suster that she go
No faster cours than ye thise yeres two.
Thanne shal she been evene atte fulle alway,
And spring flood laste bothe night and day.
And but she vouche sauf in swich manere
To graunte me my sovereyn lady deere,   400
Prey hire to sinken every rok adoun
Into hir owene dirke regioun
Under the ground, ther Pluto dwelleth inne,
Or nevere mo shal I my lady winne.
Thy temple in Delphos wol I barefoot seke.

Lord Phebus, se the teeris on my cheke,
And of my peyne have som compassioun.
And with that word in swowne he fil adoun,
And longe time he lay forth in a traunce.

410   His brother, which that knew of his penaunce,
Up caughte him, and to bedde he hath him broght.
Dispeyred in this torment and this thoght
Lete I this woful creature lie;
Chese he, for me, wheither he wol live or die.

Arveragus, with heele and greet honour,
As he that was of chivalrie the flour,
Is comen hoom, and othere worthy men.
O blisful artow now, thou Dorigen,
That hast thy lusty housbonde in thine armes,

420   The fresshe knyght, the worthy man of armes,
That loveth thee as his owene hertes lyf.
No thing list him to been imaginatif,
If any wight hadde spoke, whil he was oute,
To hire of love; he hadde of it no doute.
He noght entendeth to no swich mateere,
But daunceth, justeth, maketh hire good cheere;
And thus in joye and blisse I lete hem dwelle,
And of the sike Aurelius wol I telle.

In langour and in torment furius

430   Two yeer and moore lay wrecche Aurelius,
Er any foot he mighte on erthe gon;
Ne confort in this time hadde he noon,
Save of his brother, which that was a clerk.
He knew of al this wo and al this werk;
For to noon oother creature, certeyn,
Of this matere he dorste no word seyn.
Under his brest he baar it moore secree

94

Than evere dide Pamphilus for Galathee.
His brest was hool, withoute for to sene,
But in his herte ay was the arwe kene.   440
And wel ye knowe that of a sursanure
In surgerye is perilous the cure,
But men mighte touche the arwe, or come therby.
His brother weep and wailed prively,
Til atte laste him fil in remembraunce,
That whiles he was at Orliens in Fraunce,
As yonge clerkes, that been lykerous
To reden artes that been curious,
Seken in every halke and every herne
Particuler sciences for to lerne—   450
He him remembred that, upon a day,
At Orliens in studie a book he say
Of magik natureel, which his felawe,
That was that time a bacheler of lawe,
Al were he ther to lerne another craft,
Hadde prively upon his desk ylaft;
Which book spak muchel of the operaciouns
Touchinge the eighte and twenty mansiouns
That longen to the moone, and swich folye
As in oure dayes is nat worth a flye;   460
For hooly chirches feith in oure bileve
Ne suffreth noon illusioun us to greve.
And whan this book was in his remembraunce,
Anon for joye his herte gan to daunce,
And to himself he seyde prively:
'My brother shal be warisshed hastily;
For I am siker that ther be sciences
By whiche men make diverse apparences,
Swiche as thise subtile tregetoures pleye.

470 For ofte at feestes have I wel herd seye
That tregetours, withinne an halle large,
Have maad come in a water and a barge,
And in the halle rowen up and doun.
Somtime hath semed come a grim leoun;
And somtime floures springe as in a mede;
Somtime a vine, and grapes white and rede;
Somtime a castel, al of lym and stoon;
And whan hem liked, voided it anon.
Thus semed it to every mannes sighte.

480   Now thanne conclude I thus, that if I mighte
At Orliens som oold felawe yfinde
That hadde thise moones mansions in minde,
Or oother magik natureel above,
He sholde wel make my brother han his love.
For with an apparence a clerk may make,
To mannes sighte, that alle the rokkes blake
Of Britaigne weren yvoided everichon,
And shippes by the brinke comen and gon,
And in swich forme enduren a wowke or two.
490 Thanne were my brother warisshed of his wo;
Thanne moste she nedes holden hire biheste,
Or elles he shal shame hire atte leeste.'
    What sholde I make a lenger tale of this?
Unto his brotheres bed he comen is,
And swich confort he yaf him for to gon
To Orliens that he up stirte anon,
And on his wey forthward thanne is he fare
In hope for to been lissed of his care.
    Whan they were come almoost to that citee,
500 But if it were a two furlong or thre,
A yong clerk rominge by himself they mette,

96

Which that in Latin thriftily hem grette,
And after that he seyde a wonder thing:
'I knowe,' quod he, 'the cause of youre coming.'
And er they ferther any foote wente,
He tolde hem al that was in hire entente.

This Briton clerk him asked of felawes
The whiche that he had knowe in olde dawes,
And he answerde him that they dede were,
For which he weep ful ofte many a teere.   510

Doun of his hors Aurelius lighte anon,
And with this magicien forth is he gon
Hoom to his hous, and maden hem wel at ese.
Hem lakked no vitaille that mighte hem plese.
So wel arrayed hous as ther was oon
Aurelius in his lyf saugh nevere noon.

He shewed him, er he wente to sopeer,
Forestes, parkes ful of wilde deer;
Ther saugh he hertes with hir hornes hye,
The gretteste that evere were seyn with ye.   520
He saugh of hem an hondred slain with houndes,
And somme with arwes blede of bittre woundes.
He saugh, whan voided were thise wilde deer,
Thise fauconers upon a fair river,
That with hir haukes han the heron slain.

Tho saugh he knightes justing in a plain;
And after this he dide him swich plesaunce
That he him shewed his lady on a daunce,
On which himself he daunced, as him thoughte.
And whan this maister that this magik wroughte   530
Saugh it was time, he clapte his handes two,
And farewel! al oure revel was ago.
And yet remoeved they nevere out of the hous,

97

Whil they saugh al this sighte merveillous,
But in his studie, ther as his bookes be,
They seten stille, and no wight but they thre.

To him this maister called his squier,
And seyde him thus: 'Is redy oure soper?
Almoost an houre it is, I undertake,

540   Sith I yow bad oure soper for to make,
Whan that thise worthy men wenten with me
Into my studie, ther as my bookes be.'

'Sire,' quod this squier, 'whan it liketh yow,
It is al redy, though ye wol right now.'
'Go we thanne soupe,' quod he, 'as for the beste.
Thise amorous folk somtime moote han hir reste.'

At after-soper fille they in tretee
What somme sholde this maistres gerdon be,
To remoeven alle the rokkes of Britaine,

550   And eek from Gerounde to the mouth of Saine.

He made it straunge, and swoor, so God him save,
Lasse than a thousand pound he wolde nat have,
Ne gladly for that somme he wolde nat goon.

Aurelius, with blisful herte anoon,
Answerde thus: 'Fy on a thousand pound!
This wide world, which that men seye is round,
I wolde it yeve, if I were lord of it.
This bargain is ful drive, for we been knit.
Ye shal be payed trewely, by my trouthe!

560   But looketh now, for no necligence or slouthe
Ye tarie us heere no lenger than to-morwe.'

'Nay,' quod this clerk, 'have heer my feith to borwe.'

To bedde is goon Aurelius whan him leste,
And wel ny al that night he hadde his reste.

What for his labour and his hope of blisse,
His woful herte of penaunce hadde a lisse.

Upon the morwe, whan that it was day,
To Britaigne tooke they the righte way,
Aurelius and this magicien biside,
And been descended ther they wolde abide.   570
And this was, as thise bookes me remembre,
The colde, frosty seson of Decembre.

Phebus wax old, and hewed lyk laton,
That in his hoote declinacion
Shoon as the burned gold with stremes brighte;
But now in Capricorn adoun he lighte,
Where as he shoon ful pale, I dar wel seyn.
The bittre frostes, with the sleet and reyn,
Destroyed hath the grene in every yerd.
Janus sit by the fyr, with double berd,   580
And drinketh of his bugle horn the wyn;
Biforn him stant brawen of the tusked swyn,
And 'Nowel' crieth every lusty man.

Aurelius, in al that evere he kan,
Dooth to this maister chiere and reverence,
And preyeth him to doon his diligence
To bringen him out of his peynes smerte,
Or with a swerd that he wolde slitte his herte.

This subtil clerk swich routhe had of this man
That night and day he spedde him that he kan   590
To waiten a time of his conclusioun;
This is to seye, to maken illusioun,
By swich an apparence or jogelrye—
I ne kan no termes of astrologye—
That she and every wight sholde wene and seye
That of Britaigne the rokkes were aweye,

99

Or ellis they were sonken under grounde.
So atte laste he hath his time yfounde
To maken his japes and his wrecchednesse
600   Of swich a supersticious cursednesse.
His tables Tolletanes forth he brought,
Ful wel corrected, ne ther lakked nought,
Neither his collect ne his expans yeeris,
Ne his rootes, ne his othere geeris,
As been his centris and his argumentz
And his proporcioneles convenientz
For his equacions in every thing.
And by his eighte speere in his wirking
He knew ful wel how fer Alnath was shove
610   Fro the heed of thilke fixe Aries above,
That in the ninthe speere considered is;
Ful subtilly he kalkuled al this.
    Whan he hadde founde his firste mansioun,
He knew the remenaunt by proporcioun,
And knew the arising of his moone weel,
And in whos face, and terme, and everydeel;
And knew ful weel the moones mansioun
Acordaunt to his operacioun,
And knew also his othere observaunces
620   For swiche illusiouns and swiche meschaunces
As hethen folk useden in thilke dayes.
For which no lenger maked he delayes,
But thurgh his magik, for a wyke or tweye,
It semed that alle the rokkes were aweye.
    Aurelius, which that yet despeired is
Wher he shal han his love or fare amis,
Awaiteth night and day on this miracle;
And whan he knew that ther was noon obstacle,

That voided were thise rokkes everichon,
Doun to his maistres feet he fil anon, 630
And seyde, 'I woful wrecche, Aurelius,
Thanke yow, lord, and lady myn Venus,
That me han holpen fro my cares colde.'
And to the temple his wey forth hath he holde,
Where as he knew he sholde his lady see.
And whan he saugh his time, anon-right hee,
With dredful herte and with ful humble cheere,
Salewed hath his soverein lady deere:
 'My righte lady,' quod this woful man,
'Whom I moost drede and love as I best kan, 640
And lothest were of al this world displese,
Nere it that I for yow have swich disese
That I moste dien heere at youre foot anon,
Noght wolde I telle how me is wo bigon.
But certes outher moste I die or pleyne;
Ye sle me giltelees for verray peyne.
But of my deeth thogh that ye have no routhe,
Aviseth yow er that ye breke youre trouthe.
Repenteth yow, for thilke God above,
Er ye me sleen by cause that I yow love. 650
For, madame, wel ye woot what ye han hight—
Nat that I chalange any thing of right
Of yow, my soverein lady, but youre grace—
But in a gardyn yond, at swich a place,
Ye woot right wel what ye bihighten me;
And in myn hand youre trouthe plighten ye
To love me best—God woot, ye seyde so,
Al be that I unworthy am therto.
Madame, I speke it for the honour of yow
Moore than to save myn hertes lyf right now,— 660

I have do so as ye comanded me;
And if ye vouche sauf, ye may go see.
Dooth as yow list; have youre biheste in minde,
For, quik or deed, right there ye shal me finde.
In yow lith al to do me live or deye,—
But wel I woot the rokkes been aweye.'

He taketh his leve, and she astoned stood;
In al hir face nas a drope of blood.
She wende nevere han come in swich a trappe.
670 'Allas,' quod she, 'that evere this sholde happe!
For wende I nevere by possibilitee
That swich a monstre or merveille mighte be!
It is agains the proces of nature.'

And hoom she goth a sorweful creature;
For verray feere unnethe may she go.
She wepeth, wailleth, al a day or two,
And swowneth, that it routhe was to see.
But why it was to no wight tolde shee,
For out of towne was goon Arveragus.
680 But to hirself she spak, and seyde thus,
With face pale and with ful sorweful cheere,
In hire compleynt, as ye shal after heere:

'Allas,' quod she, 'on thee, Fortune, I pleyne,
That unwar wrapped hast me in thy cheyne,
Fro which t'escape woot I no socour,
Save oonly deeth or elles dishonour;
Oon of thise two bihoveth me to chese.
But nathelees, yet have I levere to lese
My lyf than of my body to have a shame,
690 Or knowe myselven fals, or lese my name;
And with my deth I may be quit, ywis.
Hath ther nat many a noble wyf er this,

And many a maide, yslain hirself, allas!
Rather than with hir body doon trespas?
  Yis, certes, lo, thise stories beren witnesse:
Whan thritty tirauntz, ful of cursednesse,
Hadde slain Phidon in Atthenes atte feste,
They comanded his doghtres for t'areste,
And bringen hem biforn hem in despit,
Al naked, to fulfille hir foul delit,
And in hir fadres blood they made hem daunce
Upon the pavement, God yeve hem meschaunce!
For which thise woful maidens, ful of drede,
Rather than they wolde lese hir maidenhede,
They prively been stirt into a welle,
And dreynte hemselven, as the bookes telle.

  They of Mecene leete enquere and seke
Of Lacedomye fifty maidens eke,
On whiche they wolden doon hir lecherye.
But was ther noon of al that compaignye
That she nas slain, and with a good entente
Chees rather for to die than assente
To been oppressed of hir maidenhede.
Why sholde I thanne to die been in drede?
Lo, eek, the tiraunt Aristoclides,
That loved a maiden, heet Stymphalides,
Whan that hir fader slain was on a night,
Unto Dianes temple goth she right,
And hente the image in hir handes two,
Fro which image wolde she nevere go.
No wight ne mighte hir handes of it arace
Til she was slain, right in the selve place.
  Now sith that maidens hadden swich despit
To been defouled with mannes foul delit,

700

710

720

Wel oghte a wyf rather hirselven slee
Than be defouled, as it thinketh me.
What shal I seyn of Hasdrubales wyf,
That at Cartage birafte hirself hir lyf?
For whan she saugh that Romayns wan the toun,

730 She took hir children alle, and skipte adoun
Into the fyr, and chees rather to die
Than any Romayn dide hire vileynye.
Hath nat Lucresse yslain hirself, allas!
At Rome, whan that she oppressed was
Of Tarquin, for hire thoughte it was a shame
To liven whan that she had lost hir name?
The sevene maidens of Milesie also
Han slain hemself, for verrey drede and wo,
Rather than folk of Gawle hem sholde oppresse.

740 Mo than a thousand stories, as I gesse,
Koude I now telle as touchinge this mateere.
Whan Habradate was slain, his wyf so deere
Hirselven slow, and leet hir blood to glide
In Habradates woundes depe and wide,
And seyde, "My body, at the leeste way,
Ther shal no wight defoulen, if I may."
      What sholde I mo ensamples heerof sayn,
Sith that so manye han hemselven slain
Wel rather than they wolde defouled be?

750 I wol conclude that it is bet for me
To sleen myself than been defouled thus.
I wol be trewe unto Arveragus,
Or rather sleen myself in som manere,
As dide Demociones doghter deere
By cause that she wolde nat defouled be.
O Cedasus, it is ful greet pitee

To reden how thy doghtren deyde, allas!
That slowe hemself for swich a manere cas.
As greet a pitee was it, or wel moore,
The Theban maiden that for Nichanore   760
Hirselven slow, right for swich manere wo.
Another Theban maiden dide right so;
For oon of Macidonye hadde hire oppressed,
She with hire deeth hir maidenhede redressed.
What shal I seye of Nicerates wyf,
That for swich cas birafte hirself hir lyf?
How trewe eek was to Alcebiades
His love, that rather for to dien chees
Than for to suffre his body unburied be.
Lo, which a wyf was Alceste,' quod she.   770
'What seith Omer of goode Penalopee?
Al Grece knoweth of hire chastitee.
Pardee, of Laodomya is writen thus,
That whan at Troie was slain Protheselaus,
Ne lenger wolde she live after his day.
The same of noble Porcia telle I may;
Withoute Brutus koude she nat live,
To whom she hadde al hool hir herte yive.
The parfit wyfhod of Arthemesie
Honured is thurgh al the Barbarie.   780
O Teuta, queene! thy wyfly chastitee
To alle wives may a mirour bee.
The same thing I seye of Bilyea,
Of Rodogone, and eek Valeria.'
   Thus pleyned Dorigen a day or tweye,
Purposinge evere that she wolde deye.
But nathelees, upon the thridde night,
Hoom cam Arveragus, this worthy knight,

And asked hire why that she weep so soore;
790 And she gan wepen ever lenger the moore.
'Allas,' quod she, 'that evere was I born!
Thus have I seyd,' quod she, 'thus have I sworn'—
And toold him al as ye han herd bifore;
It nedeth nat reherce it yow namoore.
This housbonde, with glad chiere, in freendly wise
Answerde and seyde as I shal yow devise:
'Is ther oght elles, Dorigen, but this?'
'Nay, nay,' quod she, 'God helpe me so as wys!
This is to muche, and it were Goddes wille.'
800 'Ye, wyf,' quod he, 'lat slepen that is stille.
It may be wel, paraventure, yet to day.
Ye shul youre trouthe holden, by my fay!
For God so wisly have mercy upon me,
I hadde wel levere ystiked for to be
For verray love which that I to yow have,
But if ye sholde youre trouthe kepe and save.
Trouthe is the hyeste thing that man may kepe'—
But with that word he brast anon to wepe,
And seyde, 'I yow forbede, up peyne of deeth,
810 That nevere, whil thee lasteth lyf ne breeth,
To no wight telle thou of this aventure—
As I may best, I wol my wo endure—
Ne make no contenance of hevinesse,
That folk of yow may demen harm or gesse.'
And forth he cleped a squier and a maide:
'Gooth forth anon with Dorigen,' he saide,
'And bringeth hire to swich a place anon.'
They take hir leve, and on hir wey they gon,
But they ne wiste why she thider wente.
820 He nolde no wight tellen his entente.

Paraventure an heep of yow, ywis,
Wol holden him a lewed man in this
That he wol putte his wyf in jupartie.
Herkneth the tale er ye upon hire crie.
She may have bettre fortune than yow semeth;
And whan that ye han herd the tale, demeth.

This squier, which that highte Aurelius,
On Dorigen that was so amorus,
Of aventure happed hire to meete
Amidde the toun, right in the quikkest strete,   830
As she was bown to goon the wey forth right
Toward the gardyn ther as she had hight.
And he was to the gardyn-ward also;
For wel he spied whan she wolde go
Out of hir hous to any maner place.
But thus they mette, of aventure or grace,
And he saleweth hire with glad entente,
And asked of hire whiderward she wente;
And she answerde, half as she were mad,
'Unto the gardyn, as myn housbonde bad,   840
My trouthe for to holde, allas! allas!'

Aurelius gan wondren on this cas,
And in his herte hadde greet compassioun
Of hire and of hire lamentacioun,
And of Arveragus, the worthy knight,
That bad hire holden al that she had hight,
So looth him was his wyf sholde breke hir trouthe;
And in his herte he caughte of this greet routhe,
Consideringe the beste on every side,
That fro his lust yet were him levere abide   850
Than doon so heigh a cherlissh wrecchednesse
Agains franchise and alle gentillesse;

For which in fewe wordes seyde he thus:
  'Madame, seyth to youre lord Arveragus
That sith I se his grete gentillesse
To yow, and eek I se wel youre distresse,
That him were levere han shame (and that were
    routhe)
Than ye to me sholde breke thus youre trouthe,
I have wel levere evere to suffre wo
860 Than I departe the love bitwix yow two.
I yow relesse, madame, into youre hond
Quit every serement and every bond
That ye han maad to me as heerbiforn,
Sith thilke time which that ye were born.
My trouthe I plighte, I shal yow never repreve
Of no biheste, and heere I take my leve,
As of the treweste and the beste wyf
That evere yet I knew in al my lyf.
But every wyf be war of hire biheeste!
870 On Dorigen remembreth, atte leeste.
Thus kan a squier doon a gentil dede
As wel as kan a knight, withouten drede.'
    She thonketh him upon hir knees al bare,
And hoom unto hir housbonde is she fare,
And tolde him al, as ye han herd me said;
And be ye siker, he was so weel apayd
That it were inpossible me to write.
What sholde I lenger of this cas endite?
    Arveragus and Dorigen his wyf
880 In soverein blisse leden forth hir lyf.
Nevere eft ne was ther angre hem bitwene.
He cherisseth hire as though she were a queene,
And she was to him trewe for everemoore.

Of thise two folk ye gete of me namoore.

Aurelius, that his cost hath al forlorn,
Curseth the time that evere he was born:
'Allas,' quod he, 'allas, that I bihighte
Of pured gold a thousand pound of wighte
Unto this philosophre! How shal I do?
I se namoore but that I am fordo.   890
Myn heritage moot I nedes selle,
And been a beggere; heere may I nat dwelle,
And shamen al my kinrede in this place,
But I of him may gete bettre grace.
But nathelees, I wole of him assaye,
At certeyn dayes, yeer by yeer, to paye,
And thanke him of his grete curteisye.
My trouthe wol I kepe, I wol nat lie.'

With herte soor he gooth unto his cofre,
And broghte gold unto this philosophre,   900
The value of five hundred pound, I gesse,
And him bisecheth, of his gentillesse,
To graunte him dayes of the remenaunt;
And seyde, 'Maister, I dar wel make avaunt,
I failled nevere of my trouthe as yit.
For sikerly my dette shal be quit
Towardes yow, howevere that I fare,
To goon a-begged in my kirtle bare.
But wolde ye vouche sauf, upon seuretee,
Two yeer or thre for to respiten me,   910
Thanne were I wel; for elles moot I selle
Myn heritage; ther is namoore to telle.'

This philosophre sobrely answerde,
And seyde thus, whan he thise wordes herde:
'Have I nat holden covenant unto thee?'

'Yes, certes, wel and trewely,' quod he.
'Hastow nat had thy lady as thee liketh?'
'No, no,' quod he, and sorwefully he siketh.
'What was the cause? tel me if thou kan.'

920   Aurelius his tale anon bigan,
And tolde him al, as ye han herd bifoore;
It nedeth nat to yow reherce it moore.
    He seide, 'Arveragus, of gentillesse,
Hadde levere die in sorwe and in distresse
Than that his wyf were of hir trouthe fals.'
The sorwe of Dorigen he tolde him als;
How looth hire was to been a wikked wyf,
And that she levere had lost that day hir lyf,
And that hir trouthe she swoor thurgh innocence,—

930   She nevere erst hadde herd speke of apparence.
'That made me han of hire so greet pitee;
And right as frely as he sente hire me,
As frely sente I hire to him ageyn.
This al and som; ther is namoore to seyn.'
    This philosophre answerde, 'Leeve brother,
Everich of yow dide gentilly til oother.
Thou art a squier and he is a knight;
But God forbede, for his blisful might,
But if a clerk koude doon a gentil dede

940   As wel as any of yow, it is no drede!
    Sire, I releesse thee thy thousand pound,
As thou right now were cropen out of the ground.
Ne nevere er now ne haddest knowen me.
For, sire, I wol nat taken a peny of thee
For al my craft, ne noght for my travaille.
Thou hast ypayed wel for my vitaille.
It is ynogh, and farewel, have good day!'

And took his hors, and forth he goth his way.
Lordinges, this question, thanne, wol I aske now,
Which was the mooste fre, as thinketh yow?   950
Now telleth me, er that ye ferther wende.
I kan namoore; my tale is at an ende.

NOTES

1–2. The Squire, the son of the Knight, has been telling a long
and excessively complicated story belonging to the genre of
chivalric romance. The Franklin interrupts him in mid-
sentence just as he has summarized the further complications
still to come, but he does so with the greatest possible polite-
ness. For more detailed comment, see Introduction, pp. 70–3.

2. *gentilly* From the very beginning, the Franklin introduces,
as part of his compliment to the Squire, the concept of
gentillesse which is to be a key element in his own story.

4. *allow the* 'praise thee'. Note the rhyme *yowthe...allow the*,
which forms part of the evidence for supposing that the final
-e, though mute in fourteenth-century speech, was pronounced
at the end of a line of Chaucerian verse.

8. *vertu* Probably with a somewhat wider sense than 'virtue'
today, meaning manly qualities in general, and thus recalling
the etymology from Latin *virtus* (cf. *vir*, 'man').

11. *twenty pound worth lond* 'land worth twenty pounds a year
in rent'.

12. 'Though it had come into my possession at this very
moment.'

16. *yet shal* 'shall continue to do so'.

23. This forthright manner of talking is characteristic of Harry
Bailly, the host of the Tabard Inn, who had been appointed
master of ceremonies for the journey by the other pilgrims.
The Franklin has already used *gentil*, *gentilly*, and *gentillesse*
once each, not to mention *vertu* (twice) and *vertuous*, and the
Host fears that he may be embarking on a moral disquisition
rather than a story.

24–6. The original proposal, made by the Host and agreed to
by the other pilgrims, was that each of them should tell two
tales on the way to Canterbury and two on the way back.
If this had been carried out, it would have resulted in an
enormous collection of some 120 stories. The vagueness here
about the number of tales to be told by each pilgrim may be
a sign that, as he proceeded with the work, Chaucer was
coming to feel that the original scheme was impossible.

46. *have me excused of* 'allow me to be excused for'.

47. *rethorik* Rhetoric was the art of eloquence, and played an important part in medieval education.

49–54. For comment and explanation, see Introduction, pp. 74–5.

57. *Armorik* Armorica, a learned name for Brittany. This line helps to set the tale in the pagan past: it 'is' (i.e. now) called Brittany.

61. *were* Subjunctive, because the outcome was uncertain.

62. *oon the faireste under sonne* An emphatic form of the superlative: 'one who was the most beautiful on earth' not 'one of the most beautiful on earth'.

63. 'And, moreover, descended from such an aristocratic family.'

64. *wel* This adds emphasis to *unnethes*, 'hardly', but cannot be translated in modern English.

68. 'Took such pity on his suffering.'

71. The line may be intended to have a sardonic ring, reflecting on the extreme theories, of male dominance and female dominance respectively, of the Clerk and the Wife of Bath.

72. 'And so as to lead their lives in greater happiness.'

73. *as a knight* 'by his knighthood'.

75. *maistrie* was a word much used by the Wife of Bath to describe the relationship between husband and wife, as was *soverainetee* (line 79 below).

78. See Introduction, pp. 19 and 21.

80. 'He wanted that, out of regard for his rank.' Presumably the *degree* concerned is that of husband, though conceivably it might be that of knight, by which he has just sworn; or it might mean that he was ashamed of his rank, which was lower than the lady's.

83–5. 'You propose to allow me so free a rein, may God never permit that there should be either hostility or quarrelling between the two of us through any fault of mine.'

87. *trouthe* The first mention of a concept that is to be very important in *The Franklin's Tale*.

89–114. A digression, in which the Franklin offers his own views on the way in which marriage may best be arranged so as to allow for inevitable human frailties. Digression is encouraged by the medieval *artes poeticae* as a means of amplifying a given story, and many of the *Canterbury Tales* include such digressions shortly after the narrative itself has begun. Their purpose is to lay explicit stress on themes which will emerge as the meaning of the story.

90. *freendes* 'lovers'.

93–4. The sudden change from abstractions such as *maistrye* to this vividly realized personification is startlingly effective. The god of love—Cupid, the son of Venus—was usually represented as winged. In the Middle Ages he is usually shown in literature as himself exercising *maistrye* over lovers.

96. *of kinde* 'by nature'.

99. *looke who* 'whoever'.

100. 'In a position of superiority above all.' The paradox is sharp: perhaps too sharp, for it does not get rid of *maistrye* but suggests a different way of achieving it.

102–3. 'For, as the scholars say, it overcomes in matters where severity would never be successful.' There is no need to identify *thise clerkes*, for it is common in medieval literature to attribute such general statements about human life (*sententiae*) to the learned. Statements making this particular point are common from the Bible onwards.

104. 'One can't scold or complain for every little word.'

105. *so moot I goon* 'I assure you'—a common and almost meaningless asseveration, literally 'As I hope to live'.

108. *that he ne dooth* 'who does not do'.

109. *constellacioun* The position of the planets in relation to each other, which was believed to influence human life. Translate 'planetary influence'.

110. *complexioun* The balance of the four humours in a person's body, which were believed to govern the health and disposition.

113–14. 'Anyone who is capable of self-control will restrain himself according to the occasion.'

115. Here Chaucer returns to his story, though he still has more discursive matter about marriage to offer before the actual narrative can continue.

120–6. The paradoxical nature of their marriage is further asserted. According to *fine amour* the woman had absolute dominion; according to marriage, as conceived in the Middle Ages, the man had absolute dominion. In this marriage, the two relationships are combined.

Notes

123. *lordshipe above* 'supreme dominion'.
126. 'With which the law of love is in agreement.'
131–4. These lines, both verbally and in their interrogative form, echo a passage in *The Merchant's Tale*.
135. The second *of* is redundant.
136. *Kayrrud* This seems to be a phonetic spelling of a genuine fourteenth-century place-name, which has now become 'Kerru'. There is more than one Kerru in Brittany, but none in the exact region where the Tale is set.
   Arveragus A Celtic name, given in a Latinized form.
138. In the Middle Ages Brittany was often called Little Britain, as opposed to Great Britain. Britain is an archaic and scholarly name for England, as Armorica for Brittany.
140. Chaucer is here repeating a chivalric theme from *The Squire's Tale*, where a female falcon tells of how she was courted by a male and accepted his advances, and how he then said he must leave her to pursue honour. In medieval chivalric romances it is generally agreed that a knight must not linger at home, even though married, but must go off in search of martial adventure.
141. *the book seith thus* There is no reason to suppose that Chaucer is really referring to a particular book. Medieval poets usually pretended to be following some authoritative source, even when they were not.
143. *Dorigen* Another Celtic name, probably pronounced with a hard *g*.
146. The tone of this line is highly dubious: is Chaucer showing an admiration for the capacity of the aristocracy to express intense emotions, or is he sardonically suggesting that noble wives have their sighing and weeping thoroughly under control?
147. Intense emotions, and especially intense grief, tend to be expressed in medieval poetry in a formalized, non-realistic way, and this line sums up the usual external symptoms of misery: yearning, wailing, lamenting, and an inability to sleep or eat.
151. *in al that ever they may* 'in every way they possibly can'.
157–9. These lines form a *sententia* which is also a miniature digression, whose connection with the main line of the narrative does not become apparent until the transition in line 160.

7   115   SFP

Notes

The saying that 'long dripping wears away the hardest stone' is a common one, and occurs in Boccaccio's *Filocolo*, a probable source for *The Franklin's Tale*. Boccaccio was translating Ovid's *Ars amatoria*, Book I, line 476 ('Yet hard rocks are hollowed out by soft water'), which would also have been known to Chaucer.

172. *derke fantasye* Fantasye is also treated as dangerous in *The Merchant's Tale*: there lustful imaginings are concerned, here melancholic imaginings.

182. *of so manye as I se* 'among all those I see'.

184. 'Completely cured of the pain of its bitter sorrow.'

206. *al be they nat in minde* 'although they are forgotten'.

208. *lyk to thyn owene merk* 'in thine own image'—repeating the language of Genesis 1:27, where the Latin *imago* is used. This is one of the basic texts for medieval Christian thought about the nature of man.

217. *as kepe* 'may (God) preserve'. The *as* is a normal means of expressing a wish or hope in Middle English.

this my conclusion 'this is *my* conclusion'. Dorigen is parodying the technical philosophical language which she attributes to *clerkes*.

222. This line has the explicitness that belongs to a poetry intended for reading aloud to a listening audience. In such poetry, the author, to make sure that the listeners (who will not possess a written text of the work) will be able to follow it, will need first to say what he is going to do (as in line 192) and then to say when he has done it.

227. *delitables* The adjective is derived from French, and it is under French influence that it agrees in number with the noun.

228. *tables* 'backgammon'—a game of chance played with dice.

229. Here begins a separate scene in the poem, in striking contrast to the previous one. For the terrifying rocky landscape of the coast is substituted the paradisal landscape of an enclosed garden. For comment, see Introduction, pp. 52–5.

234. May is the season in which the symbolic garden of love is usually described (as it is in the *Roman de la Rose*, for example), but it is not known what special significance, if any, the date of the sixth may have had for Chaucer.

235. 'And May with its gentle showers had painted.' The meta-

phor of painting is common in medieval descriptions of spring.

237. *craft of mannes hand* 'human skill'—nature and art combine to make the garden seductively beautiful.

246. Dinner in the Middle Ages would have been at midday or earlier.

260. The construction here is a confusion of that found in line 62 with the more familiar 'one of the handsomest men'.

261. *vertuous* See note on line 8.

265. *lusty* Contrary to what the context may suggest, this does not mean 'lustful' or even 'virile' but simply 'pleasant'.

    servant to Venus Venus is the goddess of love. Love relationships are commonly seen in the Middle Ages in feudal terms, so that the lover becomes the 'servant' of Venus or Cupid, or of his lady. It is precisely this feudalization from which the Tale seems to be trying to escape in its description of the relationship between Dorigen and Arveragus.

266. *Aurelius* A Roman name, which was used in Roman Britain.

269–80. Unaccepted love is normally described in medieval courtly literature as a state of intense anguish or *penaunce*. It is literally a disease, which if uncured may lead to madness and death. The symptoms are further described below, in lines 429–43.

270. *withouten coppe* A cryptic phrase, whose meaning has not been definitely ascertained. Perhaps the most likely is that suggested by Phyllis Hodgson in her edition of *The Franklin's Tale*: 'without measure, i.e. not in measured doses, but from the fountain head'.

271. *despeyred* 'in despair'. The word has theological overtones, despair of God's grace being the ultimate sin, which makes salvation impossible. *Fine amour* is often developed into a pseudo-theology, secular love being seen as a parallel to or parody of divine love. Grace is what the lover hopes to gain from his lady (compare line 286).

273. *general compleyning* 'lament in general terms'.

275. *matere* A little more specific in meaning than the modern 'matter'; it is the regular word for the subject-matter of literature as opposed to its form.

    layes 'songs'—a more general sense than in 'Breton Lays', which are narrative poems.

276. The *compleint* or lament was a common medieval literary genre. Chaucer, in his capacity as court poet, wrote a number of *compleintes*. *Roundels* and *virelayes* are both short poems whose form is based on round dances, the verses being sung by an individual and followed by refrains sung by the whole company. Their fixed form and repeated rhymes gave scope for the virtuosity that was expected of a courtier.

278. The three Furies in classical mythology were spirits which tormented the souls there, but Chaucer seems to have thought of them as suffering pain themselves.

279–80. Echo was a nymph who fell in love with the handsome youth Narcissus, and, when he did not return her love, wasted away until she became only a voice. The story is told by Ovid in the *Metamorphoses* Book III, and is repeated in the *Roman de la Rose*. Chaucer may have chosen this particular comparison as a sign of the effeminacy to which Aurelius is reduced by love.

284. Customary social events such as the ceremonies of May day or Christmas, or even as here dances, are often referred to as *observaunces*.

291. *hadde* 'she had'.

295. The oath reminds us of Dorigen's anguish about the rationale of the divine creation, and prepares us for the reintroduction of the rocks.

300. *service* 'devotion'—compare note on *servant to Venus* in line 265.

305. *as* Redundant (as frequently in Middle English).

316–26. Here Dorigen makes her fatal mistake, in a way that is all the more humanly convincing because it is unintentional and yet reveals her deepest feelings. She has too much feminine soft-heartedness to be able to hurt Aurelius (who, after all, has just declared that he loves her) by an unqualified refusal, and so she reverts from being an outraged wife to playing the part of the courtly mistress that her marriage has left open to her. Her device for evading a direct refusal will work only on condition that the task really is impossible. If it were to be performed, the very event that would open the way for her husband's safe return would also give her lover the right to possess her. And what would happen then?

320. *looke what day* 'whatever day'.

328–33. Here Dorigen reverts to the role of faithful wife, and in lines 331–3 she specifically repudiates extramarital love in the bluntest possible way.

337–9. There is perhaps an intentional note of melodrama in Aurelius's words and action, though, as has been mentioned, love was thought of as a disease that really could lead to death. However, there is no question of *sodeyn* (immediate) death, however *horrible*, for we later learn that Aurelius languishes in misery for over two years.

340. Again a skilful change of scene, with the sudden appearance of her friends, gaily ignorant of the drama that has just occurred and of Aurelius's misery.

344–6. For comment on these lines, see Introduction, p. 67.

348. Another sudden shift to a scene of contrasting emotion.

351. *colde* Verb, not adjective.

359–407. The setting of the tale is pagan, and so Aurelius prays not to the Christian God, but to the sun-god of classical paganism, Apollo. But the mythological detail of this speech is not merely antiquarianism on Chaucer's part, for the classical gods had become attached to particular 'planets' (including the sun and moon), and in the Christian Middle Ages they retained a genuine power through the belief in astrology. In this speech there is some genuine science mixed in with the pseudo-science of astrology, for of course the movements of the sea are influenced by the moon.

An invocation similar to this occurs in the *Teseida* of Boccaccio, but Chaucer was also probably influenced by the passage of Boethius used in Dorigen's earlier invocation of God. This passage (Book 1, metrum 5) is concerned with the regularity of times and seasons: it addresses God as *governour* (cf. line 359), speaks of *seedes*, *leeves*, and *cornes* (cf. line 360), and begins with a reference to the moon and *hir brother* (cf. line 373) the sun.

For further comment on this speech, see Introduction, p. 45–6.

364. *Phebus* Phoebus is a name applied to Apollo in his role as sun-god.

365. *which that am but lorn* 'who am utterly lost'.

367. *withoute gilt* 'without any fault of mine'. *but* 'unless' (followed by a verb in the subjunctive, *have* not *hath*).

benignitee Apollo, according to medieval astrology, was the most favourable of the planet-gods in influence, and was therefore sometimes called *Fortuna major*.

373. *Lucina* One of the names of the threefold goddess Diana. She is Diana, the goddess of hunting and chastity on earth, Luna, the moon, in heaven, and Proserpina in the underworld. As Lucina she is the goddess prayed to for help by women in childbirth. For further information, see *The Knight's Tale*, ed. Spearing, lines 1193–228 (the description of the temple of Diana). It has been suggested that Aurelius has to adopt the roundabout approach of asking Apollo to ask his sister to make the sea rise because he knew that, as Diana, she was the goddess of chastity, and would have been unlikely to perform a miracle to enable him to seduce another man's wife.

375–6. Neptune was the god of the sea itself, but the sea's movements were controlled by the influence of the moon.

377–8. The moon shines with light reflected from the sun. This scientific fact was known in the Middle Ages, but it is interesting to see here how it is humanized, and made a matter not simply of neutral reflexion but of desire and the kindling of fire.

379. This presumably refers to the fact that night continually succeeds day, and so the moon the sun.

385–6. *The Leon* is Leo, the lion, one of the twelve 'houses' of the zodiac, the belt across the sky within which the sun and the other planets move in their courses. The sun is especially associated with the house of Leo, and is at its most powerful when within it. In May, when Aurelius makes his prayer, the sun is in another house, Taurus, the bull, and he will have to wait three months for the sun to be in Leo. At that time the moon will be 'in opposition' to the sun (that is, they will be 180 degrees apart at full moon), and this is one of the arrangements which causes the tides to be highest, because the sun influences them as well as the moon.

387. *as* See note on line 217.

393. What has been requested so far is in the course of nature, but what Aurelius goes on to ask for is indeed a miracle, for it involves making the moon move at the same apparent rate as the sun for two years (i.e. revolving round the earth once a year instead of once a month), so as to keep the same

exceptional spring tide in being. His science appears to be mistaken, however, for this miracle would not produce the effect he desires.

399. *but she vouche sauf* 'if she will not consent'.

401–3. This will be within her powers as Proserpina or Hecate, goddess of the underworld, which is ruled over by the god Pluto.

405. *Delphos* A confusion of Delos, where Apollo was born, and Delphi, where his chief oracle was. Aurelius, in medieval fashion, is vowing a barefoot 'pilgrimage' to this shrine if his prayer is answered.

413. *lete I...lie* 'I leave...lying'.

414. 'So far as I am concerned, he can make up his own mind whether he is going to live or die.'

438. *Pamphilus* and *Galathee* (Galatea) are characters in a medieval Latin poetic dialogue, *Pamphilus de Amore*.

439–43. The metaphor of love as a wound received in the breast (or heart) from an arrow is common in medieval courtly poetry. It is found in the influential *Roman de la Rose*, and also in the opening lines of *Pamphilus de Amore*. It is often treated literally, so that, as here, the means of curing the wound can be discussed in technical medical terms. Thus the *sursanure*, or wound healed over on the surface, becomes an image for the passion of love kept secret.

445–56. The Franklin is trying to convey too much information in a single sentence, and changes grammatical construction (drawing breath, as it were) halfway through.

446. *Orliens in Fraunce* Brittany was a duchy separate from France in Chaucer's time, but Bretons used regularly to go and study at the University of Orleans.

448. 'To study esoteric sciences.' At universities today, students are still sometimes spoken of as 'reading' particular subjects, not 'studying' them. This is the first suggestion of magic in the poem.

451. *Remembred* is here used as a reflexive verb; compare modern French *il se souvint*.

452. *at Orliens in studie* 'while he was studying at Orleans'.

453. *magik natureel* There was a clear distinction in the Middle Ages between 'natural magic' and necromancy or 'black magic'. Natural magic was a science which brought power through a special knowledge of natural phenomena (such as,

in this case, planetary influences), while necromancy made use of evil spirits, and was universally condemned.

454. *bacheler of lawe* An advanced student who has not yet taken his master's degree. Orleans was famous for the study of law in the Middle Ages, but it was also known as a centre of astrology.

457–9. The twenty-eight *mansiouns* of the moon are the positions in which it appears on each of the twenty-eight days of the lunar month. In each position it had a different kind of influence, and so a knowledge of these positions was of great value for someone who wished to predict or change the future.

459–62. Another withdrawal from involvement in the tale: we are reminded that we are Christians, while the tale belongs to the errors of a pagan past. If we think of this remark as being the Franklin's, it sounds perhaps somewhat anxious— he is concerned to assert his own respectable orthodoxy. If we think of it as Chaucer's, it takes on a more quizzical air, a little sceptical that *hooly chirches feith* is so all-powerful. The Wife of Bath at the beginning of her tale makes some similar remarks about how the *grete charitee and prayeres* of the friars have abolished fairies, and these too must be understood ironically.

461. 'For the faith of Holy Church in our creed.'

470–9. Conjuring tricks of this kind were used as entertainments at feasts in Chaucer's time.

470–1. *for ofte...that tregetours* 'for I have certainly heard it said that often at feasts conjurers'.

479. This line emphasizes the element of seeming in magic; the changes caused by magicians only appear to be so.

481. *oold felawe* 'former companion (of mine)'.

485–6. Further emphasis on the illusory nature of magic.

493. Such indications that the writer intends to be brief are very common in Chaucer and other medieval poets. The *artes poeticae* sometimes divide the possible purposes of poetry into two, to amplify the given material and to abbreviate it, and the poets tend to be very conscious which of the two they are doing. The following sentence is indeed extraordinarily concise; in line 494 he is still approaching his brother's bed with his new idea, and in line 498 the two of them are already on the way to Orleans to carry it out.

Notes

500. 'No more than some two or three furlongs away.' A furlong is one-eighth of a mile (about 200 metres).

507–8. The brother is hoping to carry out his original plan (lines 480–1) of making contact with some former friend of his who knows about natural magic.

513. *maden hem* 'they made themselves'.

515–16. 'Never in his life had Aurelius seen a house so well provided as that one was.'

517–29. For comment, see Introduction, pp. 63–4.

529. *as him thoughte* 'as it seemed to him'. Again the emphasis on the illusory nature of magic, now at a crucial point, when Aurelius seems to be achieving what he most desires.

535. *ther as his bookes be* This clause, as its recurrence in line 542 indicates, is little more than the kind of time- and space-filler that belongs to the diffuse style of a poem intended for oral delivery. But, though a formula, it has a certain significance here, for it is presumably his books that have enabled him to create the illusions.

545. *as for the beste* 'as the best thing to do'. Another space-filler.

546. *thise amorous folk* 'people in love'.

550. The Gironde and the Seine are rivers almost equally far from Penmarc'h on opposite sides.

551. *so God him save* 'as he hoped to be saved'—a common oath.

556. It was regularly taught in the Middle Ages that the earth was round, not flat.

562. *have heer my feith to borwe* 'take my promise as a pledge'. They make their agreement with legal formality.

571. *thise bookes* See note on line 141.

573–83. These lines, deriving from a literary and rhetorical tradition, form an extremely elaborate periphrasis for the statement that it was in December. But they are also related to a visual tradition. They form a literary equivalent for the illuminations in medieval Calendars and Books of Hours (the best known example today being probably *Les Très Riches Heures du Duc de Berry*), in which the upper part of the picture will show the astronomical situation for a month (lines 573–7), while the lower part will contain a typical scene from life in the same month (lines 578–83). Janus is the god of the turn of the year, and he is sometimes shown in illustrations of January (the month called after him) but sometimes also in those of December. The feasting scene is shown in illustrations of several winter months, but is particularly appropriate to the Christmas feast, which in medieval times lasted from 25 December to 6 January. Thus the rhetorical significance of this passage is clear, and so is its imaginative vitality: it stands out from its surroundings as brilliantly coloured and full of vigorous life. It seems possible to see it as representing a promise that the forces of evil or illusion will not win: even in the *colde, frosty seson of Decembre*, so ominously chosen for the experiment, a vigorous and familiarly English life survives, and even in this pagan world Christian possibilities can be glimpsed. But equally Janus *with double berd* is a fundamentally ambiguous figure, looking both back and forward, hinting perhaps at both good and evil.

573–7. In summer the sun shines powerfully from a high altitude (*declinacion*) in the sky; at the winter solstice, when it is in the zodiacal house of Capricorn (compare note on lines 385–6), it is duller in colour and shines only palely.

580. *with double berd* Janus is often shown with two faces looking in opposite directions. Here these are merely alluded to in the double beard, and he becomes a hearty human figure, perhaps in the image of the Franklin himself, who was much given to good food.

581. *bugle horn* The horn of the bugle or wild ox was used as a drinking vessel.

582. A boar's head was a ceremonial dish for Christmas festivities, and is also often shown in January illuminations in medieval Calendars.

583. *Nowel* (from Latin *natalis*, 'birthday') was shouted aloud at the Christmas festivities.

588. 'Or (he begged) that he would pierce his heart with a sword.'

591. 'To be on the watch for an opportunity for his experiment.'

594. With this modest parenthesis, compare the *diminutio* in lines 44–55. As there, it is immediately followed by an ostentatious display of knowledge. Here, though, it is only the *termes* of astrology of which knowledge is shown: what the scientific process really involves remains mysterious.

600. *supersticious* This does not imply 'illusory', but rather

'diabolic'. Both kinds of magic, natural and 'black', were believed in in the Middle Ages, though only natural magic was approved of by the orthodox. There has so far been no definite indication that the Clerk is employing anything but natural magic; but when used by a pagan this too is tainted with paganism.

601. *tables Tolletanes* Astronomical tables were necessary for the practice of astrology, and the most widely used ones (on which Chaucer based his own *Equatorie of the Planetis*) were the Alfonsine tables, drawn up for the longitude of Toledo in Spain (hence *Tolletanes*) in the thirteenth century.

602. *corrected* Tables based on the longitude of Toledo would have to be modified for use in Brittany.

603–4. The *root* of a set of tables is the first date for which figures are given. A table for *collect* years is one enabling calculations to be made for long periods of time, from twenty years upwards, while a table for *expans* years gives figures for shorter periods of time. The two together would enable a planet's positions in any given year to be calculated.

605. *as been* 'such as'. *centris* The centres of the various circles in which the planets move. *argumentz* The angles governing a planet's position in its epicycle.

606. *proporcioneles convenientz* Figures for calculating the positions of planets during fractions of a year.

607. *equacions* Corrections to take account of minor motions.

608–11. According to the cosmology derived by the Middle Ages from Aristotle, the physical universe was arranged in nine concentric spheres, with the earth at the centre, and the Primum Mobile, which gave motion to all the rest, at the outside. The 'fixed' stars (i.e. those which were not planets) were in the eighth sphere. The twelve houses of the zodiac were usually measured in the ninth sphere, and took their names from the constellations with which they had originally coincided. Thus Alnath, a star in the constellation of Aries (the Ram), would originally have coincided with the zodiacal house of Aries. But the eighth sphere was in slow rotation (a fact which explained the precession of the equinoxes), and so the two no longer coincided. The Clerk knew how far they had moved apart, and took account of this in his calculation.

613. *firste mansioun* The first mansion (see note on lines 457–9) of the moon, which was called Alnath.

616. Each house of the zodiac was divided into equal parts called *faces* and into unequal parts called *termes*, and each *face* and *terme* was assigned to a particular planet. *Whos* therefore might refer either to a sign of the zodiac or to a planet.

617–18. Chaucer does not tell us which *was* the appropriate mansion of the moon for the experiment; we are evidently to be impressed without understanding. The next few lines are much vaguer.

632. Venus here does not seem to be 'astrologized', but to refer to the goddess of love.

652–3. Here the parody theology of love is used: just as man obtains salvation not by right but through God's free grace, so Aurelius begs for Dorigen's love. But there is something sinister in his modesty; he is keeping to the letter of the theology of love, but his whole speech *is* claiming her love as something due to him according to her promise.

671–3. Previously Dorigen had thought of the rocks as a *monstre*, something unnatural; now she thinks of their removal as such. Despite her earlier speech, complaining about the ordering of the universe, it appears now that she does after all believe in a natural order, a *proces of nature*, against which this magical illusion is an offence.

683–6. Dorigen begins another formal *pleynt* with an arraignment of Fortune, comparable with her earlier arraignment of God and his providence. Fortune is an important figure in medieval thought, and one of the seminal works behind the medieval conception of her is Chaucer's favourite *Consolation of Philosophy* of Boethius. Book II of the *Consolation* develops an elaborate image of Fortune as the force in control of all worldly events, dealing out prosperity and misery quite arbitrarily, and not according to men's deserts. She is visualized as a woman turning a great wheel, on which men rise and then fall. The chain that Dorigen here refers to is no doubt that by which men are attached to the wheel.

695–784. For comment on this list of twenty-two *exempla*, see Introduction, pp. 55–7.

696. At the end of the Peloponnesian War, the Thirty Tyrants seized power in Athens, murdering Phidon and instituting a tyranny.

707. 'The men of Messene had inquiries and searches made.'

711. *that she nas* 'who was not'.

715. Aristoclides was ruler of Orchomenos in Arcadia.

718. Diana was goddess of chastity. See note on line 373.

727–8. Hasdrubal was king of Carthage, the great rival city to Rome, when it was sacked by the Romans in the third Punic war.

730. *skipte* Judgements of the tone of words in fourteenth-century English are bound to be uncertain, but this word sounds light-hearted, in a way which undercuts the seriousness of the speech.

733–6. The story of Lucretia has become better known than most of the other *exempla*, partly no doubt through the influence of Shakespeare's poem *The Rape of Lucrece*. She was raped by Tarquin, and then committed suicide so as not to bring dishonour to her husband. Is it significant that Dorigen has now introduced an *exemplum* of a woman who killed herself *after* being raped, rather than before? Does it mean that this possibility has entered her own mind, or simply that she is becoming confused by her distress?

737–9. Miletus was sacked by the Gauls in the third century B.C.

742–6. Abradates was king of the Susi.

746. *if I may* 'if I can help it'.

754–5. Demotion's daughter killed herself when her fiancé died, so as not to be forced to marry someone else.

756–8. The daughters of Scedasus killed each other after being raped.

759–61. Nichanor was an officer of Alexander's at the capture of Thebes.

763. *for oon of Macidonye* 'because a man from Macedonia'.

765–6. The wife of Niceratus killed herself after her husband had been put to death by the Thirty Tyrants of Athens, so as to avoid falling into their hands herself. The case is remote from Dorigen's, though her vague *for swich cas* does something to conceal the fact.

767–9. Timandra, Alcibiades's mistress, insisted on burying his body after he had been murdered by the Thirty Tyrants.

768. *rather for to dien chees* 'chose rather to die'.

770. Alcestis died in place of her husband, Admetus.

771–2. Penelope was the wife of Odysseus; during his long absence, as recounted in the *Odyssey* of Homer, she was much

pestered by suitors who took him to be dead, but she resisted
them and he eventually returned.

773–5. When Protesilaus was killed by Hector at Troy, his
wife Laodamia voluntarily accompanied him to the underworld.

776–8. Portia killed herself through anxiety about her husband
Brutus.

779–80. Artemisia built a great sepulchre, or mausoleum, for
her dead husband Mausolus. It is difficult to see what Dorigen
could learn from the story.

781–2. Despite the double emphasis of *wyfly...wives*, it appears that Teuta was not married. Dorigen's *exempla* are
becoming more and more desperately irrelevant. The idea of
taking an event as a *mirour* (Latin *speculum*) or pattern for
one's own life is a common one in medieval literature, which
rarely fails to draw an explicit moral from a story.

783–4. Bilia showed her *parfit wyfhod* by putting up with her
husband's bad breath; Rhodogune killed her nurse for trying
to persuade her to marry a second time; Valeria refused to
marry a second time.

793–4. As is natural in a poet writing for an audience of
listeners, Chaucer manipulates his subject-matter explicitly,
and, instead of simply not repeating himself, tells us that he
is not going to repeat himself.

797. His reaction is startlingly mild—the very opposite of what
we should expect. Dorigen's reply indicates her surprise.

798. *God helpe me so as wys!* Literally 'so indeed may God
help me!'.

799. *and* 'if'.

800. Compare the proverb 'Let sleeping dogs lie'. Arveragus
evidently sees Dorigen's agitated comment as the prelude to
a recapitulation of the whole story, her feelings of guilt, etc.,
and wishes to avoid all this.

801. *paraventure* Pronounced (here but not in line 821) 'paraun-
ter'. This line is no doubt intended as a warning to *us* that the
ending is not necessarily going to be tragic or even shameful, a
warning which Chaucer amplifies in lines 821–6. But there can
be no guessing what in particular Arveragus is referring to in
it—presumably it is intended merely as vague reassurance.

803. 'For as surely as I hope God will have mercy on me.'

807. *thing* This word seems to have here something of its older meaning of 'contract'.

808. His hitherto repressed emotion at last breaks out. But we shall perhaps be surprised to find that it is the thought of his reputation that produces his tears: he is concerned not with what is going to happen to his wife, but with what people will think of him. The reaction is in keeping with his initial stipulation that he must have *the name of soverainetee* in marriage, but see Introduction, pp. 35–7.

814. 'So that people can suspect or guess any evil of you.'

821–6. A brief digression, in which Chaucer directly addresses his audience—a common feature of poetry intended for oral delivery.

833. 'And he was also on his way to the garden.' Verbs of motion can sometimes be omitted in Middle English.

837. *with glad entente* 'in happy expectation'.

840. Thus she openly admits her husband's *maistrie*, though paradoxically it has been exercised to give her up to another man.

851–2. The *cherlissh* is the exact opposite of the *gentil*. *Cherlissh* behaviour is what you would expect of a *cherl*, a lower-class person, while *gentillesse* is the ideal behaviour of an aristocrat. *Franchise* has approximately the same meaning as *gentillesse*, except that it implies more specifically generosity of behaviour.

854–60. In this extremely complicated sentence, 'and eek I se wel youre distresse' seems likely to be a parenthesis, with the sense carrying straight on from *gentillesse to yow* to *that him were levere*.

857. *him were levere han shame* 'he would rather be (publicly) humiliated'.

861–2. 'My lady, I return into your hands, as if discharged, every oath and every agreement.' Aurelius here and in the next two lines uses the legal language of a medieval release or quitclaim. See Introduction, pp. 28–9.

869–72. It is not clear (since quotation marks were not used in medieval manuscripts) whether these words are part of Aurelius's speech or whether they form a narratorial comment on the situation. In the light of the similarity in phrasing between lines 871–2 and the Clerk's boast in lines 939–40 (which are unquestionably spoken by the Clerk himself), it seems most likely that these lines too are spoken by the person to whom they refer.

869. 'But let every wife be careful what she promises!'

890. 'For all I can see, I am ruined.'

894. 'Unless I can obtain more mercy from him.'

897. *curteisye* Another of the key medieval ethical concepts is here introduced, along with *gentillesse, franchise,* and *trouthe*.

899. In the Middle Ages, it was normal for personal wealth to be stored in material form (such as gold, as here) in an iron-bound chest.

903. 'And allow him time to pay the balance.'

905. 'So far I have never failed to keep my word.'

908. 'Even if I go begging in my bare tunic.'

909. Having granted Dorigen a formal quitclaim, Aurelius is now trying to come to another legal arrangement with the Clerk.

921–2. Compare lines 793–4. This is clearly a formula of abbreviation, which the audience will understand as such, rather than a sign of poverty of language. The idiom of poetry intended to be read aloud will necessarily contain a large formulaic element, especially among the machinery of story-manipulation.

925. *were of hir trouthe fals* 'failed to keep her word'.

932–3. *Fre* (see line 950) and *frely* are the adjective and adverb corresponding to the noun *franchise* (see line 852 and note).

938–9. 'But God in his blessed power forbid that a scholar should not be able to perform a noble deed.'

942. Literally, 'as if you had crept out of the ground this very minute'—that is, as if you had just been born. Again a legal quitclaim is granted, though in somewhat fanciful language.

949–52. It was common for medieval poems of a courtly kind to end with an explicit question; Chaucer brings Part I of *The Knight's Tale* to an end in the same way. Here the purpose of the convention is particularly clear: where poetry is a form of communal entertainment, a pastime, it will fulfil its function most satisfactorily when it provides matter for discussion among the listeners when a particular poem is at an end. In this case we do not hear any discussion of the poem among the other pilgrims, such as we find elsewhere in *The Canterbury Tales*, because *The Franklin's Tale* is at the end of one of the manuscript fragments, and is not linked with any succeeding material.

GLOSSARY

abegged begging
abide (inf. *abiden*) wait, stay,
  abstain
above (l. 483) in addition
accord agreement
acordaunt appropriate
acordeth (inf. *acorden*) agrees
adoun down
after after, afterwards;
  according to
again(s) against; back
ageyn back
al all; (followed by subjunctive verb) although; (l. 206)
  al be they although they are;
  (l. 455) *al were he* although
  he was; (l. 658) *al be that I*
  although I
Alcebiades Alcibiades
Alceste Alcestis
aleyes garden paths
allow (inf. *allowen*) praise
Alnath a star in Aries
als also
alwey constantly
amidde in the middle of
amonges among
amor(o)us in love
and and; (l. 799) if
ano(o)n at once; *anon-right*
  immediately
anoyeth (inf. *anoyen*) does
  harm
apaid (inf. *apayen*) pleased
apparence(s) illusion(s)
Appollo Apollo
arace (inf. *aracen*) tear away

argumentz see note on l. 605
aright correctly
arising rising
Armorik Armorica (a name for
  Brittany)
array dress
arrayed (inf. *arrayen*) adorned,
  arranged
artes sciences
Arthemisie Artemisia
artow (inf. *been*) art thou
arwe(s) arrow(s)
as as (if). Often redundant,
  especially in relative con-
  structions
assaye (inf. *assayen*) attempt
asterte (inf. *asterten*) escape
astoned dumbfounded
aswage (inf. *aswagen*)
  diminish
atte at the
atteyne (inf. *atteynen*) over-
  come
Atthenes Athens
avantage (l. 100) *at his avantage* in a position of
  superiority
avaunt boast
aventure fortune; event
aventures happenings
aviseth (inf. *avisen*) *aviseth
  yow* consider
awaiteth (on) (inf. *awaiten*)
  watches (for)
ay always
baar (inf. *beren*) carried
bad (inf. *bidden*) ordered

Barbarie barbarian lands

bare (l. 48) unadorned

barge vessel

be (inf. *been*) been

been are, be

beest animal

berd beard

beren bear

beste best; (l. 545) *as for the beste* as the best thing to do

bet better

biforn before, in front of

bigon(ne) (inf. *biginnen*) began; (l. 644) *me is wo bigon* I am troubled by misery

bihe(e)ste promise

bihight(e)(n) (inf. *biheten*) promised

biholde (inf. *biholden*) look

bihoveth it is necessary (with dative pronoun)

bileve creed

Bilyea Bilia

birafte (inf. *bireven*) deprived

biseche(th) (inf. *bisechen*) beseech(es)

biside by his side; (l. 230) *ther biside* near there

bisily diligently

bisinesse care, diligence

bitide (inf. *bitiden*) happen

bittre bitter, cruel

bitwix(e) between

biwreye (inf. *biwreyen*) reveal

blake black

blede (inf. *bleden*) bleed

blisful joyful; (l. 373) blessed

blisse happiness

bond agreement

boot boat

borwe (l. 562) *to borwe* as a pledge

bown prepared

brast (inf. *bresten*) burst out

brawen flesh

breste (inf. *bresten*) break

bresting breaking

breyde (inf. *breyden*) (l. 355) *out of his wit he breyde* he went out of his mind

brid bird

bringeth (inf. *bringen*) (l. 817) conduct

Britai(g)ne, Briteyne Brittany; Britain

Briton Breton

Britouns Bretons

bugle horn drinking horn

burel plain

burned burnished

but but; merely; (followed by subjunctive verb) unless; *but if* unless, except

cam (inf. *comen*) came

Cartage Carthage

cas matter, situation, reason

caught(e) (inf. *cacchen*) (l. 68) taken; (l. 848) conceived

cause (l. 44) *by cause* because

causelees without cause

Cedasus Scedasus

centris centres

certein, certeyn (adj.) (l. 194) sure; (l. 896) *at certeyn dayes* on fixed days

certein, certeyn (adv.) certainly

certes indeed

chalange (inf. *chalangen*) claim

chaunce fortune

chaunginge change

cheere countenance, behaviour; (l. 426) *maketh hire good cheere* entertains her *chees* (inf. *chesen*) chose

cherisseth (inf. *cherissen*)
cherishes

cherlissh ignoble, ungracious

chese (inf. *chesen*) choose

cheyne chain

chiere countenance, expression; (l. 585) *dooth...chiere
and reverence* behaves
pleasantly and respectfully

chiertee love

chivalrie knighthood

clene free

cleped (inf. *clepen*) called

clerk(es) scholar(s)

cofre chest

colde (adj.) gloomy

colde (inf. *colden*) (l. 351)
grow cold

collect see note on ll. 603–4

colours see Introduction,
p. 74

comen (inf. *comen*) come,
descended

compaignye company; (l. 91)
holden compaignye keep
company

complaine (inf. *complainen*)
lament

compleint(es) laments

complexioun disposition (see
note on l. 110)

compleyning lament

comth (inf. *comen*) comes,
arrives

comune (inf. *comunen*) converse

conclusio(u)n (l. 217) summing
up; (l. 342) result of discussion; (l. 591) experiment

confort (l. 154) consolation;
(l. 495) encouragement

conforten (inf. *conforten*) comfort

considered (inf. *consideren*)
observable

constellacioun see note on l.
109

constreyned (inf. *constreynen*)
forced, compelled

contenance expression

contrarien oppose

contree country

coome (inf. *comen*) came

coost coast

coppe cup

corrected adapted, modified

cost expenditure

cours course

craft skill, art

crie (inf. *cryen*) (l. 824) *upon
her crie* condemn her

cropen (inf. *crepen*) crept

curious occult, esoteric

curiously elaborately

cursednesse wickedness

curteisye courtesy

dauncen (inf. *dauncen*) dance

dawes days

day(es) day(s); *day ne night* at
any time; (l. 903) *dayes of*
time to pay

declinacion altitude

dede dead

dedly dying

dees dice

defaute fault

defoulen defile

degree status

delit pleasure

delitables delightful

Delphos Delphi

Glossary

demen (l. 814) *demen harm* suspect evil

demeth (inf. *demen*) judge

Demociones Demotion's

departe (inf. *departen*) part, split

derke dark, gloomy

descended (inf. *descenden*) (l. 570) *been descended* got down

desdeyn (l. 28) *haveth...in desdeyn* be offended with

despende (inf. *despenden*) waste

despeyred, despeired in despair

despit (l. 699) cruelty; (l. 723) contempt

destreyneth (inf. *destreynen*) torments

dette debt

devise (inf. *devisen*) describe

deyde (inf. *dyen*) died

deye (inf. *dyen*) die

deyntee (*of*) pleasure (in)

Dianes Diana's

diligence (l. 586) utmost

dirke dark

disconfort distress

discrecioun discernment

discrive (inf. *discriven*) describe

disese sorrow

dispeyred in despair

disport recreation

disporte (inf. *disporten*) amuse

disputison disputation

diverse various

do (inf. *doon*) cause (to), make; (l. 306) *do me deye* cause me to die; (l. 384) *do...do* perform...make

doghtres daughters

doom (ll. 5, 256) *as to my doom* by my judgement

doon do, perform, commit

dooth (inf. *doon*) do(es)

dorste (inf. *durren*) dared, durst

doute fear

drede (noun) fear; *withouten drede, it is no drede* without doubt

drede (inf. *dreden*) fear, reverence

dredful fearful

dreynte (inf. *drenchen*) drowned

drive (inf. *driven*) (l. 558) completed

drough (inf. *drawen*) drew, approached

duren remain

ech each

eek also

eft again

eighe eye

eighte eighth

eke also

Ekko Echo

elles, ellis else

emperisse empress

emprented (inf. *emprenten*) imprinted

emprenting impression

emprise undertaking

endelong all along

endite (inf. *enditen*) write

endure(n) last

Engelond England

enquere (inf. *enqueren*) inquire

ensamples examples, *exempla*

entende (inf. *entenden*) (l. 17) apply himself

entendeth (inf. *entenden*) pays attention

134

Glossary

entente (ll. 287, 310) meaning; (ll. 506, 820) plan; (l. 711) will; (l. 837) expectation

equacions see note on l. 607

er(st) before

ese ease, comfort

eterne eternal

evene uniformly

everich every, each

evericho(o)n everyone

everydeel every bit

expans see note on ll. 603–4

eyen eyes

fader father

fadme fathoms

fadres (l. 701) father's

fantasye fantasies, imaginings

fare (inf. *faren*) gone; (l. 907) get on; *fare amis* be unlucky

faringe (l. 260) *beste faringe* handsomest

faste close

fasteth (inf. *fasten*) does not eat

fauconers falconers

feeleth (inf. *feelen*) (l. 55) *feeleth noght* understands nothing

feelingly perceptively

feendly fiendish

feere fear

feestes feasts

feith faith

felawe companion

fer(ther) far(ther)

feste feast

figure image

fil(le) (inf. *fallen*) fell; (l. 69) *fil of his accord* came to an agreement with him; (l. 292) *fille in speche* struck up conversation; (l. 445) *him fil in*

remembraunce it came into his memory; (l. 547) *fille they in tretee* they began negotiating

fir fire

firste (l. 3) original

fixe fixed

flood flood-tide

flour(es) flower(s)

folwen follow

folweth (inf. *folwen*) follows

for for; because; (l. 72) *for to* so as to

forbede (inf. *forbeden*) forbid

fordo (inf. *fordoon*) ruined

forlorn (inf. *forlesen*) completely lost

forme appearance

forth forward, out; (l. 292) continually; (l. 831) *forth right* direct

forthward forward

foul ugly

franchise generosity

Fraunce France

freendes friends; (l. 90) lovers

fre(ly) generous(ly)

fresshe bold; bright

fressher livelier

fro from

ful very

furius raging

fy fie

Galathee Galatea

gan (inf. *ginnen*) began (often used as an auxiliary verb to indicate the past tense)

Gawle Gaul

geeris equipment

gentil noble (see Introduction, pp. 31–43)

gentillesse noble behaviour,
magnanimity (see Introduction, pp. 31–43)
gentilly nobly (see Introduction, pp. 31–43)
gerdon reward
Gerounde Gironde
gesse (inf. *gessen*) suppose
gilt fault, guilt
giltelees guiltless
glade (inf. *gladen*) cheer
glide (inf. *gliden*) flow
go (inf. *goon*) go, walk
gon (inf. *goon*) gone
gonne (inf. *ginnen*) began
go(o)n go, pass, walk; (l. 553)
proceed; (l. 105) *so moot I
goon* I assure you
goon (inf. *goon*) (ll. 349, 679)
gone
go(o)th (inf. *goon*) go(es)
governaunce (l. 114) self-control; (l. 194) control
grace mercy, favour; (l. 894)
bettre grace more mercy
graunte (inf. *graunten*) consent,
allow
grave (inf. *graven*) buried
graven engrave
greet, grete great
grette (inf. *greten*) greeted
gretteste greatest
grevaunce distress
greve (inf. *greven*) harm
grisly horrible
Habradate Abradates
halke nook
han (inf. *ha(ve)n*) have
happe(d) (inf. *happen*)
chance(d), occur(red)

Hasdrubales Hasdrubal's
hastily quickly
hastow (inf. *ha(ve)n*) hast thou
haukes hawks
heed head
heele prosperity
heep lot
heerbiforn before this
heere (adv.) here
heere (inf. *heeren*) hear
heerof of this
heet (inf. *hoten*) called
heigh high; (ll. 63, 101) noble;
(l. 177) *an heigh* above;
(l. 851) great
hem them
hemself, hemselven themselves
hente (inf. *henten*) seized
herberwe position
herd(e) (inf. *heren*) heard
here (l. 118) her
heritage inheritance
herkneth (inf. *herknen*) listen to
herne cranny
heste promise
hethen heathen
hevinesse grief
hevy gloomy
hewe colour, brightness
hewed coloured
hight (inf. *hoten*) promise(d);
(l. 852) made her promise
hir(e) her; their
hirselven herself
his his, its
holde (inf. *holden*) held
holden (inf. *holden*) held;
keep; (l. 822) consider
holdeth (inf. *holden*) keep
holpen (inf. *helpen*) helped

hom home
hond hand
hool whole, wholly; (l. 439) unwounded
hooly holy
hoom home
hoote hot
housbonde husband
humblesse humility
hye(ste) high(est)
idel vain
illusioun (l. 592) deception
imaginatif suspicious
inpossible (adj.) impossible
inpossible (noun) impossibility
ire anger
jalousie jealousy
japes tricks
jogelrye conjuring
jolier gayer
jupartie danger
justeth (inf. *justen*) jousts
justing jousting
kalkuled (inf. *kalkulen*) calculated
kan (inf. *konnen*) can, am able, know; (l. 43) *as I kan*, (l. 326) *in al that evere I kan* as best I can; (l. 114) *kan on* is capable of; (l. 584) *in al that evere he kan* in every possible way; (l. 590) *that he kan* as much as possible
kene sharp
kepe (inf. *kepen*) keep, preserve
kinde nature
kinrede kindred, family
kirtle tunic
kithe (inf. *kithen*) show
knit (inf. *knitten*) (l. 314)
bound by marriage; (l. 558) agreed
knowe (inf. *knowen*) known
knowes (noun) knees
koude (inf. *konnen*) could
Lacedomye Lacedaemonia, Sparta
lakked (inf. *lakken*) there was lacking (with dative pronoun); (l. 514) *hem lakked* they lacked
langour sickness
langwissheth (inf. *langwisshen*) endures pain
Laodomya Laodamia
large unrestricted
lasse less
lat (inf. *leten*) let
laton copper
layes (l. 275) songs
lede(n) (inf. *leden*) lead
ledest (inf. *leden*) governest
leeste least; *at the leeste wey* at least; (l. 870) *atte leeste* at the very least
leet(e) (inf. *leten*) allowed; (l. 707) *leete enquere and seke* had inquiries and searches made
leeve dear
leiser opportunity
lenger longer; (l. 790) *ever lenger the moore* continually more and more
leo(u)n lion; (l. 386) Leo, a sign of the zodiac (see note on ll. 385–6)
lerneth (inf. *lernen*) learn
lese (inf. *lesen*) lose
leste (adj.) least
lest(e) (verb) see *list(e)*
lete (inf. *leten*) leave, let

lette (inf. *letten*) hinder

leve (inf. *leven*) leave off, give up

levere rather; (l. 20) *hath levere* prefers; (l. 688) *have I levere* I prefer; (ll. 850, 857) *him were levere* he would prefer; (l. 859) *I have wel levere* I would greatly prefer

leves (noun) leaves

lewed ignorant, stupid

lighte (inf. *lighten*) descended; (l. 511) *doun of . . . lighte* got down from

liketh (inf. *liken*) it pleases; (l. 146) *whan hem liketh* when it pleases them, when they please

lisse relief

lissed (inf. *lissen*) relieved

list(e), *lest(e)* (no inf.) (usually with dative pronoun) desire, wish, like

listeth (no inf.) (usually with dative pronoun) desires, wishes, likes

lith (inf. *lyen*) lies; (l. 665) *in yow lith al* it lies entirely in your power

live (l. 260) *on live* alive

lond land

longen belong

looke(th) look; see (to it); (l. 320) *looke what* whatever

looth hateful (with dative pronoun); (l. 847) *looth him was* he was unwilling

lordinges gentlemen

lordshipe mastery, dominion

lorn (inf. *lesen*) lost

lothest most unwilling

Lucresse Lucretia

lust pleasure, desire

lusty (l. 265) pleasant; (l. 419) gallant; (l. 583) jovial

lyf life

lyk like

lykerous eager

lym lime, mortar

maad (inf. *maken*) made

Macidonye Macedonia

maden (inf. *maken*) (they) made

maidenhede virginity

maister expert

maistres (l. 548) expert's

maistrie, maistrye domination

make (inf. *maken*) make, create, cause, perform

maner(e) manner, way, kind (of)

mansioun(s) station(s) (see note on ll. 457–9)

mate(e)re matter(s); (l. 275) theme

may (no inf.) may, can; (l. 746) *if I may* if I can help it

Mecene Messene

mede meadow

meenes instruments

meke humble

men people; one

mente (inf. *menen*) meant

merciable merciful

merk image

merveille marvel

merveillous marvellous

meschaunce misfortune

meschaunces cursed acts

Milesie Miletus

mirour mirror, example

mo more

monstre unnatural thing

Glossary

moone complaint

moorneth (inf. *moornen*) mourns, yearns

moot(e) (no inf.) must

morwe morning; (l. 229) *morwe-tide* time of morning

moste must

muchel much

myn my, mine

myselven myself

name name, reputation

namely especially

namoore no more

Narcisus Narcissus

nas (inf. *been*) was not

nat not

nathelees nevertheless

naturelly by its nature

ne not, nor

necligence negligence

nedes necessarily

nedeth (inf. *neden*) (it) is necessary

Neptunus Neptune

nere (inf. *been*) were not

Nicerates Niceratus's

Nichanore Nichanor

nis (inf. *been*) is not

noght nothing; not at all; (l. 149) *sette at noght* valued at nothing

nolde (inf. *willen*) would not

noon none; nobody; not

nought nothing

Nowel see note on l. 583

ny nearly

o one

obeisaunce submissiveness

observaunces customary rites

ofte often

oght anything

oghte (inf. *owen*) ought

Omer Homer

oold former

oon one

operacioun (l. 618) experiment

operaciouns (l. 457) working

opposicion see note on ll. 385–6

oppresse(d) (inf. *oppressen*) violate(d)

ordinaunce arrangements

orisonte horizon

orisoun prayer

Orliens Orleans

oute away

outher either

overspringe (inf. *overspringen*) rise above

owene own

pacient long-suffering

page servant

paine (l. 58) *dide his paine* took trouble

paraventure perhaps

parcel part

pardee indeed (a common mild oath)

parfit perfect

particuler out of the way

passinge surpassing

Pedmark Penmarc'h

peere equal

Penalopee Penelope

penaunce suffering

Pernaso Parnassus

peyne pain, sorrow; (ll. 184, 302) *peynes smerte* pain of sorrow; (l. 809) *up peyne of* on pain of

peynte(d) (inf. *peynten*) paint(ed)

Phebus Phoebus (Apollo)

philosophre scientist

pitee pity, compassion

Glossary

pitous sorrowful

pitously pitiably

plain field of contest

plesaunce pleasure, delight

pley (noun) jest

pleye(n) play; amuse (themselves); (l. 469) perform

pleyn plain

pleyne (on) (inf. *pleynen*) complain (against)

pleyneth (inf. *pleynen*) laments

pleynt lamentation

plighte(n) (inf. *plighten*) pledge(d)

Porcia Portia

possibilitee (l. 671) *by possibilitee* by any possibility

prechen (inf. *prechen*) exhort

preieth (inf. *preyen*) pray

preise (inf. *preisen*) commend

preyde (inf. *preyen*) begged

preyeth (inf. *preyen*) begs

prively secretly; (l. 69) in private; (l. 456) covered up

proces process; (l. 157) *by proces* gradually

profre propose (for)

proporcioneles convenientz see note on l. 606

proporcioun adjustment

Protheselaus Protesilaus

prys excellence; (l. 262) esteem

pured (inf. *puren*) refined

purposinge intending

purveiaunce providence; (l. 232) provisions

queynte strange

quik alive

quiked (inf. *quiken*) kindled

quikkest busiest

quit (ll. 691, 862) discharged

quod (inf. *quethen*) said

rage madness (of sorrow)

raving delirium

redden (inf. *reden*) read

reden (l. 448) study

redressed (inf. *redressen*) avenged

reft (inf. *reven*) robbed of

regioun realm

reherce (inf. *rehercen*) repeat

reine rein

rele(e)sse (inf. *relessen*) remit, return; (l. 941) set free

remembraunce memory

remembre (inf. *remembren*) remind

remenaunt remainder

remoeved (inf. *remoeven*) moved

remoeve(n) remove

repreve (of) (inf. *repreven*) reproach (about)

resoun reason

respiten grant respite

rethorik rhetoric

revel revelry

reverence respect

reweth (inf. *rewen*) have pity

reyn rain

right (adv.) just, exactly, directly; (l. 12) *right now* at this very moment

righte (adj.) direct; true

rigour severity

rimeyed written in rhyming verse

river (l. 524) hawking ground

Rodogone Rhodogune

rokkes rocks

Romayn(s) (the) Roman(s)

romen (l. 171) *romen hire* wander about

rominge wandering
rootes see note on ll. 603–4
roundels see note on l. 276
routhe (a) pity
rude rough
said (inf. *seyn*) (l. 875) say
Saine Seine
salewed (inf. *salewen*) greeted
saleweth (inf. *salewen*) greets
saufly safely
saugh (inf. *seen*) saw
save (preposition) except (for)
save (inf. *saven*) maintain
say (inf. *seen*) saw
sayn see *seyn*
Scithero Cicero
se (inf. *seen*) see
secree secretly
see sea
seen see
seeth (inf. *seen*) sees
seide (inf. *seyn*) said
seigh (inf. *seen*) saw
seillinge sailing
seith (inf. *seyn*) says
seke(n) search
selve same, very
semed (inf. *semen*) (it) seemed
  (with dative pronoun); appeared
semen (inf. *semen*) seem
sene see; (l. 439) *withoute for
  to sene* to look at from outside
serement oath
servage subjection
service devotion
seten (inf. *sitten*) sat
seuretee security
sey(e)(n) (inf. *seyn*) say
seyde (inf. *seyn*) said
seyn (inf. *seen*) (l. 520) seen

seyn, sayn say, tell, repeat
seyth (inf. *seyn*) say
shame (noun) shame, humiliation; *for shame of* out of
  regard for
shame(n) (verb) put to shame
sheene bright
sholde (inf. *shullen*) should
shoon (inf. *shinen*) shone
shoop (inf. *shapen*) (l. 137)
  shoop him arranged,
  planned
shopen (inf. *shapen*) arranged
shortly briefly
shoures showers
shove (inf. *shoven*) moved
  forward
shul (inf. *shullen*) shall; must
sike sick
siker(ly) certain(ly)
sikes sighs
siketh (inf. *siken*) sighs
sin since
sires (ladies and) gentlemen
sit (inf. *sitten*) sits
sith since
sixte sixth
skipte (inf. *skippen*) leapt
slake (inf. *slaken*) abate
sle(e)(n) kill
sleep (inf. *slepen*) (have) slept
sleeth (inf. *sleen*) kills
slide (inf. *sliden*) slip away
slitte (inf. *slitten*) pierce
slouthe laziness
slow(e) (inf. *sleen*) killed
smerte pain
snybbed (inf. *snybben*) scolded
so so, such; *so that* if
sobrely gravely
socour aid
sodeyn(ly) immediate(ly)

softe gentle

solas comfort, pleasure, delight

somme (noun) sum

somme (pronoun) some

songe (inf. *singen*) sang

sonken (inf. *sinken*) sunk

sonne sun

soor (l. 899) heavy

soore deeply, bitterly

sooth (the) truth

sope(e)r supper

sorwe(ful) sorrow(ful)

sothe truth

soupe (inf. *soupen*) have supper

soverainetee supremacy

soverein supreme

spak (inf. *speken*) spoke, said

spedde (inf. *speden*) (l. 590)
  spedde him hastened

speere sphere

squier squire

stable immutable

stant (inf. *standen*) stands

stirt(e) (inf. *stirten*) sprang,
  leapt

stoon stone

stories histories

straunge (l. 551) *made it
  straunge* held off

stryf quarrelling

Stymphalides Stymphalis

stynten cease (talking)

subtil(e) expert

subtilly expertly

suffise (inf. *suffisen*) be capable

suffraunce forbearance

suffre (inf. *suffren*) endure, be
  patient, permit

suffreth (inf. *suffren*) (l. 462)
  permits

supersticious diabolic

sursanure wound healed over
on the surface

sustene (inf. *sustenen*) keep up

suster sister

swerd sword

swich(e) such

swoor (inf. *sweren*) swore

swowne swoon

swyn boar

taak (inf. *taken*) take

tables backgammon

take (inf. *taken*) taken

tarie (inf. *tarien*) delay

teeris tears

temperaunce moderation, self-
  restraint

thanne then

the(e) thee

thennes thence, from there

ther there, where

therby near it

therto moreover; of it

thider there, to it

thilke the same, that

thing thing; contract; *no thing*
  not at all

thinketh (inf. *thinken*) it seems
  (with dative pronoun)

this this (is)

thise the; these

tho then

thogh though

thoght thought, care,
  melancholy

thonketh (inf. *thonken*) thanks

thoughte (inf. *thinken*) it
  seemed (with dative
  pronoun)

thral slave

thridde third

thriftily politely

thritty thirty

thurgh through

Glossary

thyn thy, thine

time time; (ll. 294, 591) opportunity; (l. 113) *after the time* according to the occasion

tiraunt(z) tyrants

to to; too

Tolletanes Toledan

tonge language

touchinge concerning

toun town, city

travaille labour

tregetour(e)s conjurers

trespas sin

tretee negotiation

trewe faithful

trewely truly

Troie Troy

trouthe (pledged) word; (l. 87) *have heer my trouthe* I hereby promise

turned (inf. *turnen*) (l. 339) *turned him* went away

tweyne two

under (l. 437) within

undertake (inf. *undertaken*) declare

unnethe(s) hardly

unresonable contrary to reason

untrewe unfaithful

unwiting (of) unknown (to)

usage habit

useden (inf. *usen*) practised

venquisseth (inf. *venquissen*) overcomes

verray, verrey real, very, true

vertu virtue; but see note on l. 8

vertuous accomplished

vileynye dishonour (see Appendix to *An Introduction to Chaucer*)

virelayes see note on l. 276

vitaille food

voided (inf. *voiden*) (they) dismissed

vouche(th) sauf (inf. *vouchen sauf*) grant, consent

waiten watch out for

waketh (inf. *waken*) stays awake

wan (inf. *winnen*) (had) conquered

war wary, careful

warisshed (inf. *warisshen*) cured

wax (inf. *wexen*) grew

weel well

weep (inf. *wepen*) wept

wel (a vague intensifier) well, highly, certainly, completely, very, much; (l. 64) *wel unnethes* hardly

welfare well-being

welles springs

wende (inf. *wenden*) travel

wende (inf. *wenen*) expected

wene (inf. *wenen*) imagine

were (inf. *been*) were, would be

werk work; (l. 434) trouble; (l. 313) *word ne werk* word or deed

werre hostility

whan when; *whan so that* whenever

what what; why; *what for* what with

wheither whether

wher whether; *wher so* whether

where where; *where as* where(ver)

which which, who(m), what (a)

whiderward where

whiles while

143

wight person

wighte (l. 888) *of wighte* by weight

wirking motion

wise way, manner

wisly certainly, surely

wiste (inf. *witen*) knew

wit(tes) intelligence, understanding; (l. 355) mind, wits

withal also

withoute from outside

wo misery; (l. 335) *wo was*, unhappy was; (l. 644) *me is wo bigon*, I am troubled by misery

wol(e) (inf. *willen*) will, wish to

wolde(n) (inf. *willen*) would, wished to

wonder wonderful

wondren (on) wonder (at)

woost (inf. *witen*) knowest

woot (inf. *witen*) know

worshipe (l. 139) glory; (l. 290) reputation

worthinesse excellence

worthy noble, excellent

wowke week

wrapped (inf. *wrappen*) entangled

wrecche wretched

wrecchednesse wretched work or deed

wreken (inf. *wreken*) avenged

wreye (inf. *wreyen*) disclose

wro(u)ght(e) (inf. *werchen*) did, performed, made, produced

wyf(ly) wife(ly)

wyfhod wifeliness

wyke week

wyn wine

wys (adj.) prudent, wise

wys (adv.) indeed; (l. 798) *God helpe me so as wys* God help me indeed

yaf (inf. *yeven*) gave

ye (disyllable = noun) eye

ye (monosyllable = pronoun) you

yeer(is) year(s)

yerd garden

yet still

yeve(st) (inf. *yeven*) give(st)

yfinde (inf. *(y)finden*) find

yfostred (inf. *fostren*) nourished, benefited

yfounde (inf. *finden*) found

yit yet

yive (inf. *yeven*) given

yknowe (inf. *yknowen*) recognize

yknowen (inf. *knowen*) known

ylaft (inf. *leven*) left

ynogh, ynow enough

yoore, of time yoore since old times

ypayed (inf. *payen*) paid

yquit (inf. *quiten*) (reflexive) acquitted yourself

ysene visible

yslain (inf. *sleen*) killed

ystiked (inf. *stiken*) stabbed

ysworn (inf. *sweren*) sworn

yvoided (inf. *voiden*) removed

ywis indeed, surely